The
Condo/Co-op
Owner's
Survival Manual

The Condo/Co-op Owner's Survival Manual

Harry M. Matthews, Jr.

A Perigee Book

For Bob Roberts, who always said

I should be in real estate.

This book is designed to provide accurate and authoritative information regarding condominium or co-op ownership. It is sold with the understanding that neither the author nor the publisher is engaged in rendering legal, accounting, or other professional services. Before buying or selling a condominium or co-op, the reader is encouraged to seek the services of a competent professional.

Perigee Books
are published by
The Putnam Publishing Group
200 Madison Avenue
New York, NY 10016

Library of Congress Cataloging-in-Publication Data

Matthews, Harry M.
   The condo/co-op owner's survival manual / by Harry M. Matthews, Jr.
      p.   cm.
   Includes index.
   ISBN 0-399-51632-8 (trade paperback)
   1. Condominiums—United States—Handbooks, manuals, etc.
2. Condominium associations—United States—Handbooks, manuals, etc.
3. Housing, Cooperative—United States—Handbooks, manuals, etc.
I. Title.
HD7287.67.U5M38 1991   90-39150 CIP
643'.2—dc20

Printed in the United States of America

1   2   3   4   5   6   7   8   9   10

Acknowledgments

I wouldn't have much to write about if I had not served two terms on the board of my co-op with such dedicated, energetic, and truly nice people as Barbara Delfyett-Hester, Ludlow Beckett, Angela Ferrante, and Ed Covington. Also an important part of the team was our superintendent, Eliseo Perez. Among the managers who taught us positive lessons were Ann Studen, Tom Hagan, and Larry Malitzky; those who taught us negative lessons shall remain anonymous.

My efforts to learn about the experience of others in shared-ownership housing were made a true pleasure by the willingness of many residents, board members, and managers to offer time, advice, and hospitality, particularly Dick Bogosian, David Donaldson, Jon Lonoff, Jim Johnson, Jerry Carlson, Mary Kirkland, Steve Neil, Ann Rice, Craig Murphy, and JoAnn Yates. Thanks to the Backroom and Gaycom for communications help and to Joe Rigo for bracing doses of good sense.

Don Mahan, Len Evans, Tom Raleigh, Dick Boehm, and Carol Silverman read drafts of the manuscript, saving me from countless errors and idiocies. I am particularly indebted to Professor Silverman, who generously shared the insights she has gained through several years of research in the field. Paul Conner didn't even see this project started, but he taught me so much about how organizations work, how to study them, and how to explain them clearly that I know I would never have finished without his example.

Along Publishers' Row, I enjoyed the advice and support of Diana Finch, an agent who proves that genuine enthusiasm and seasoned expertise can indeed go hand in hand, while at Perigee Books, Adrienne Ingrum, Ginger Marino, and their colleagues moved the project from manuscript to finished book with admirable dispatch.

Despite all this terrific help, I remain, of course, the sole author and responsible for all errors and oversights. If you spot mistakes, have suggestions, or want to share an experience, drop me a line, c/o Perigee Books, 200 Madison Avenue, New York, NY 10016. With your additional input, I can make the next edition more useful for all of us!

Contents

Introduction:

A New Kind of Homeowner

"Congratulations, you now own an apartment!" "Welcome to the Apex Homeowners Association!" With words like these, a handshake, and a depleted bank account, you leave the ranks of renters or house-owners and enter the burgeoning ranks of condominium, co-operative, and planned-development unit owners. You're in good company: Across the country, "shared-interest" housing has been the fastest-growing type of home ownership in recent years. In 1982 (the latest year's estimate available), more than ten million Americans lived in such developments, and the upward trend has continued. California alone claims more than sixteen thousand associations, with memberships ranging from a dozen families to thousands of individuals.

The forces behind this trend are clear and well documented. The cost of the average home has risen much faster than average family income, making the dream house in the suburbs an impossible dream for many. At the same time, more and more people—from "empty-nest" retirees to young couples gentrifying older urban neighborhoods—are discovering the appeal of town house and apartment living. To make shared-interest housing even more attractive, unit owners enjoy virtually the same hefty tax and financial advantages enjoyed by other homeowners.

But shared ownership is not the same as owning a house. Many financial, legal, social, and practical questions arise: How can you be sure your financial interests are protected? Who pays to fix leaky plumbing? What if the lobby decor reminds you of a bordello? What steps can help defuse tensions among the joint owners? I've had to answer these questions personally, as a shareholder and board member in a multiethnic co-op in one of Brooklyn's rapidly changing brownstone neighborhoods. Like many recent purchasers, my neighbors and I are first-time buyers, with no prior experience in real estate. From readings and from conversations with other owners from Boston to Berkeley, I discovered that the challenges and frustrations we have experienced are shared by millions of others. Drawing on this fund of firsthand knowledge, I have tried to make this book a survival manual for the rapidly growing ranks of unit owners across the country.

I begin with a review of the essentials: What, legally speaking, constitutes a condo, a co-op, a planned community? How are they organized? What are the principal variations on these basic themes? What are the advantages and disadvantages of the different types of ownership? Here, too, are some practical tips on what to look for and look out for when buying and selling, including special notes for tenants and buyers in buildings being converted from rental units.

Often overlooked in discussions of shared ownership are the intangible, everyday problems. Living in an apartment house makes you feel like a tenant, but you are also an owner. Even in a town house development or planned community of detached houses, it's difficult to determine where the association's responsibility stops and personal responsibility begins. For example, do you pay an association employee to fix a broken window, or is this service a routine part of the staff's job? And if you need to pay, how much?

As a homeowner, you expect to control the use and appearance of your home in order to protect your investment. But shared ownership divides these responsibilities, too. To whom do you complain about an error or omission in the financial records? If you have an idea for an improvement, whom do you approach? And who follows through on your proposal?

The heart of the book addresses the key questions of physical and fiscal management. This responsibility falls first on the board, which has considerable discretion in running the development: overseeing maintenance, hiring contractors, and, not incidentally, setting budgets and determining common charges. What qualifications mark a good board candidate? What should a newly elected board member expect? I'll discuss specific strategies for approaching the board's work: establishing basic policies, tracking routine maintenance, scheduling capital improvements, maintaining communications (the fuller the better), organizing meetings (time-consuming but essential), and encouraging advisory and support committees (to keep up the garden, for example). Special sections cover the pros and cons of common issues, such as permitting owners to rent their units and regulating alterations. And there's advice on handling the sometimes contentious relationship with the sponsor in a complex undergoing conversion from rental to shared ownership.

The board's first decision is to select a strategy for day-to-day management of the property: direct management by the board, hiring a full-time site manager, or engaging an outside firm to run the development. Factors like the size of the complex, age and condition, location, financial and human resources all need to be weighed. I'll deal with the pros and cons of each of these basic choices and with related issues like establishing realistic expectations, evaluating potential managers, negotiating a management contract, hiring and supervising employees and contractors, dealing with labor unions, and finding the kind of legal and financial advice every association needs.

Either out of fear of numbers or on the assumption that "management" takes care of money by some magical process, many owners and even board members fail to realize the realities and risks involved in community finances. Chapter 5 explains the sources of funds available and the implications of each funding technique for board members, shareholders, and the future of the building.

Real-life examples—with names and other details

changed to protect the privacy of individuals involved—
show how owners and managers have dealt with common
problems. You'll also find samples of key documents, with
commentary and definitions of the terms, and a guide to
further sources of information. The object is to give you the
tools you need to solve common problems and enjoy a well-
run community.

A NOTE ON TERMINOLOGY

There is, alas, no one concise word for the type of home
ownership I am describing here. Among professionals in
the field, the term *common-interest housing association* has
become the standard; it's accurate but cumbersome. On a
day-to-day basis, you're likely to hear "condo," "garden
apartments," "co-op," "planned community," "homeowners association," or one of a dozen other terms, depending
on local law and custom.

The various ownership structures are explained in
the next chapter, but my research has convinced me that the
basic needs and common problems are substantially the
same, regardless of the legal details of an association's
structure. As with any investment, for example, it's important to understand how your money is being spent. Like any
homeowner, you have to sort out the complexities of maintenance. And as in any group where people come together
for a common purpose, a large degree of cooperation is required to make it work. Therefore, I will use terms like
condo, association, complex, and *community* interchangeably. On the occasions when I discuss issues particular to
one type of ownership, I will emphasize the limited nature
of the advice: You can assume that all other comments apply to any form of common ownership.

Similarly, I use the term *board* in a generic sense, regardless of what title (like Board of Directors, Board of
Managers, or Administrative Council) your governing documents may use. These are the people charged with the responsibility for making and enforcing policies governing the
use and maintenance of the building. If your building is
small, in fact, the board includes all members. In the same

vein, terms like *building, complex, property, association,* and *development* are used interchangeably to describe the organization as a whole, and the people who live there may be *unit owners, members,* or *residents.* In short, consider this book a conversation among friends, not a conference among lawyers.

One additional point of potential confusion: I use the terms *manager, site manager,* and *general manager* to refer to the individual responsible for administrative and financial operations on a day-to-day basis. The person in charge of physical maintenance (and direct supervision of the staff, if any) I call the *custodian, chief engineer,* or *superintendent.* Some developments use other titles or even combine these functions in one job; I make the distinction because it is useful in describing building management responsibilities.

1
The Basics:

How Condos and Co-ops Are Organized

When Americans faced the challenge of the frontier, they banded together to build forts, raise barns, and protect common interests. Today, faced with breathtaking land and construction costs, more and more Americans are banding together to share ownership of apartment buildings, town house complexes, office blocks, and common facilities surrounding single-family homes. While there are various legal structures for this sort of banding together, the principles are the same: pooled capital for buying and building, shared responsibility for upkeep and improvement, shared benefits from tax breaks and buying supplies, like heating oil, at bulk rates. This chapter explains how these principles are applied in practice, and what a newcomer to shared ownership needs to know to evaluate a potential purchase.

THE "MICROGOVERNMENT"

Every common-interest association is run by an elected board with considerable power to set rules and control finances. In smaller developments, it might resemble a meeting of neighbors coming to terms with shared problems. In larger developments, it takes on many of the powers associated with local government. Indeed, some authorities have dubbed them "microgovernments."

These quasi-governmental powers are the source of both the advantages and the disadvantages found in all kinds of shared-interest housing. On the plus side, decisions affecting the value of your property and your everyday life are made directly by you and your neighbors, not in some distant council or legislature. But the decisions can be more sweeping and more arbitrary, and, without sound leadership, factionalism and personality conflicts can split an association and lead to paralysis.

CO-OPERATIVES

The oldest of the modern forms of shared ownership is the *co-operative*. Under this arrangement, the property is owned by a corporation whose only shareholders are its residents. The legal structure is analogous to that of a rental building, but the landlord consists of the tenants as a whole, united in the co-op corporation. Technically speaking, co-operators do not own their units, but portions of the "indivisible whole" of the entire property. Each resident owns a block of shares, porportional to the size of his or her unit, and has a *proprietary lease* "tied" to those shares and conveying the right to live in that particular unit on a long-term basis.

For many years, co-operatives were looked on as very exclusive housing, built mainly for the rich. This largely outdated stereotype was rooted in three facts. First of all, the earliest large-scale co-ops were indeed built to attract wealthy families at a time when town house living was losing its social cachet. At the same time, banks were reluctant to grant loans for co-op purchases, since the collateral was not real property but stock in the co-operative corporation. Buyers, therefore, had to have the full purchase price in cash—a condition only the wealthy could meet. Finally, all applicants had to submit to screening interviews with the governing board, which could exclude anyone who didn't "belong," such as people who went to the "wrong" church or whose forebears came from the "wrong" country.

At the same time, co-ops were being developed as a way

to provide affordable housing to moderate-income families. Established under special state and federal laws, these complexes were generally constructed with subsidized or government-guaranteed loans and operated on a strictly nonprofit basis. In this case, shareholders are not permitted to sell the apartments on the open market; if they choose to leave, they must resell their shares to the co-op at same price they originally paid. To qualify for an apartment in such a complex, a family must have an income below an established ceiling—as well as a lot of patience, since they usually have extremely long waiting lists.

Today, in those parts of the country where they are common, co-ops are designed to fit a wide variety of incomes and life-styles. Bank loans are readily available, and the board's exclusionary powers—seldom invoked in any event—are further limited by civil rights laws. Some disadvantages remain: Board screening can delay a sale, and a conservative board may reject an applicant whose finances are marginal. In addition, co-op loans carry somewhat higher interest rates than conventional mortgages, reflecting the slightly greater difficulty the bank would encounter in liquidating its collateral in the event of foreclosure. It is also somewhat more difficult and costly to borrow against your equity in a co-op.

On the plus side, board screening does reduce the risk of individual shareholders getting stuck with making up the loss from neighbors who default. The fact that there is only one owner of the entire complex (the co-operative corporation) means that shareholders can pay insurance, taxes, and maintenance costs in one conveniently consolidated monthly payment. For the same reason, the co-op corporation may be able to borrow money in its own name for improvements, enabling co-operators to defer payments over many years and to benefit from the tax-deductibility of the interest.

CONDOMINIUMS

Although condominium ownership was unknown in this country before 1960, it has now become the most popular form of shared-ownership housing in America. Under a condo plan, residents hold legal title to their units, as if they were freestanding houses. In addition, they own a pro-portional share of "common elements," like lobbies, yards, roofs, and recreational facilities. And while the word *condo* conjures up images of luxury high-rise towers, condomini-ums actually come in a wide range of sizes and styles, in-cluding town houses, garden apartments, and even freestanding houses sharing private streets or courtyards.

The advantages are virtually identical to those of home ownership. You can buy or sell the unit with few restric-tions and finance it or borrow against its value on the same terms as any other piece of real property. Condo rules usu-ally allow considerable freedom to rent or remodel the unit. Contrary to popular belief, though, a condo board *does* have the power to regulate alterations, restrict sublets, and even, to an extent, control or block resales. These tools for pro-tecting the common interests of all unit owners are, how-ever, less sweeping than those of a co-op board and are likely to be exercised with greater restraint.

The disadvantages mirror a co-op's advantages. The less stringent screening of buyers somewhat increases the possibility that an owner might default, an expense even-tually shared by all owners. While legal structures and lo-cal customs vary, the fact that the association may own no property in its own name makes it difficult—often impos-sible—for a condo to borrow funds. As a result, capital im-provements must be financed out of accumulated reserves or by imposing special assessments directly on unit owners. (For more details, see Chapter 5, "Money Matters.") Taxes and insurance—along with the added paperwork and record-keeping requirements—are the responsibility of in-dividual unit owners. Condo developments often attract ab-sentee owners who plan only to sublet rather than live in the building; under such circumstances, it becomes diffi-cult to create a sense of community, and a disproportionate share of management tasks falls on the resident unit owners.

PLANNED COMMUNITIES

A planned community might be thought of as a condo without an apartment house. Members usually own freestanding houses or town houses that share amenities—private streets, a swimming pool, a golf course, or just a unique, distinctive appearance—whose maintenance and improvement are undertaken by a homeowners association. Membership in the association is usually part of the property deed, requiring any owner of the house to join and support the association's activities. Finances are similar to those of a condo, in that members are required to pay regular assessments, on a monthly or sometimes quarterly basis, to cover the upkeep of the shared facilities.

Such associations are especially good examples of microgovernments, since they take such "municipal" responsibilities as providing recreational facilities or restricting the number, type, and architectural style of buildings on each lot. Indeed, planned communities are particularly popular in areas where local government resources are limited or where there are no zoning laws or land-use controls.

RETIREMENT CONDOS AND CO-OPS

These developments start out with the basic organization of a co-op or condominium, then add special features, such as maid service or nursing facilities. Some even provide a form of insurance, promising buyers lifetime care in an onsite nursing home, if needed. These offerings have only recently come on the market, so it's difficult to predict how well they will work in practice. The primary considerations, of course, are the same as with any other purchase of a home. But the financial implications of the retirement "extras" must be carefully evaluated in light of each individual's personal situation. Don't sign anything until you've discussed it with an accountant, lawyer, or other financial advisor.

COMMERCIAL CONDOMINIUMS

Another recent innovation, these developments permit small and medium-sized businesses to own their own offices or factories as part of a condominium. The structure of the organization and the risks and benefits involved are quite similar to those of residential condos, with a few exceptions. Financially, small businesses are notoriously unstable, and defaults are therefore a greater risk than in residential condos. Prospective buyers, therefore, should pay particular attention to the default provisions in the governing documents and should look into the financial status of fellow owners. Decision making, on the other hand, is often easier, especially when all the unit owners are in the same or related businesses. Some commercial condos hold meetings by circular memo, permitting unit owners to comment or vote on key issues without the inconvenience of a face-to-face meeting.

ORGANIZATION AND DOCUMENTS: THE KEY ELEMENTS

As soon as you express serious interest in buying into a shared-interest community, you must confront "The Book," an imposing set of documents which set up the legal and operational framework for shared ownership. Chapter 6 contains more detailed information, but this outline introduces the institutions and documents you'll be dealing with. The precise names vary with local law and custom, but I've given the most common ones in parentheses. Whether condo, co-op, or planned community, every development has these elements:

1. A charter establishing shared ownership (prospectus, charter, declaration, master deed), which precisely describes the property owned and the legal framework within which it is shared. In some states, this document will also

include financial disclosures about the developer, schedules of expenses and income, a report on the physical condition of the building, and a statement of the development's cash reserves and projected needs. If the development is being converted from a rental, this document may also detail any protections offered to nonpurchasing rental tenants.

2. A legal entity (the corporation, the association, the condominium), which provides the framework for joint action and is the formal owner of any property held in common—the entire building in the case of a co-op, building systems and common areas in a condo, shared amenities in the case of a planned community. Each member owns a part of this entity, often in proportion to the size of his or her individual units.

3. Rules governing the functions of the corporation or association (by-laws, regulations, association rules), which establish the governing body, define its powers, determine how and when membership meetings must be called, and generally regulate the internal operations of the association or corporation.

4. A governing body (board of directors, board of trustees, board of managers, council), which is elected by the owners to establish and implement management policies. (If there are fewer than a dozen unit owners, all the members often become, de facto, the board.)

5. A manager (managing agent, site manager), who is responsible for day-to-day operations and routine paperwork. In medium-sized and larger complexes, this is usually an outside firm hired for its expertise in real estate. In small developments, one of the unit owners may take this role. (See Chapter 4, "Day-to-Day Management," for more details.)

6. Rules governing the relationship between individual owners and the entity (proprietary lease in a co-op; association rules, regulations, conditions, covenants, and restrictions elsewhere), which spell out the division between individual and collective rights and responsibilities. These regulations are difficult to amend and will probably play the largest role in determining your personal and financial satisfaction; read them with special care.

7. Rules governing relations among individual owners

(house rules), which are really a form of institutionalized politeness, cover issues like whether or not pets are allowed, when music can and cannot be played, whether laundry should be carried in the passenger elevator, where cars should and should not be parked. These rules are fairly easily amended, but they do represent an established consensus that members may be reluctant to disturb.

WHAT A BUYER SHOULD LOOK FOR

Assuming the neighborhood, the property, and the unit itself are attractive to you, consider the following points:

1. *Fundamental questions.* Read "The Book" and make sure first that you understand the rules and terms it contains and second that you can live comfortably with them. Your lawyer should read it as well, but you should get the information firsthand, relying on the lawyer principally to point out potential trouble spots and answer specific questions from you.

2. *Financial questions.* Ask for financial statements from the past two full years to learn more about the development's financial condition; the seller should be able to furnish you with these reports. Is the complex running at a surplus or a deficit? How often have common charges been raised? Has the building done a survey of future cash needs for both regular upkeep and capital improvements? What plans does it have to fund these needs? Is there a substantial cash reserve? If not, is one being built up?

3. *Physical questions.* How sound are the service systems? Pay particular attention to the roof, wiring, plumbing, windows, and, in cold-weather regions, the boiler—the systems that are the most expensive to fix. If a major improvement is needed, when will it occur and how will it be financed? Don't depend entirely on a real estate agent; ask to see board minutes covering these issues. Alternatively, you or your lawyer should discuss these questions with a board member. You can also conduct your own examination of key building systems, preferably in the company of an engineer, a knowledgeable friend, or following a checklist in a book on sound house construction.

If the unit itself needs work—repainting, say, or a new bathtub—this is a matter to negotiate with the *seller*. Neither the board nor the manager has any authority in relations between buyer and seller and therefore cannot make good on any failure to stick to an agreement reached before the sale. No matter how reassuring the seller may sound, insist on getting a list of the all the agreed upon improvements explicitly stated in the contract of sale. This step preserves your right to call the deal off if the specified work isn't done. As Sam Goldwyn is supposed to have said, "A verbal contract isn't worth the paper it's printed on."

4. *Personal questions.* Before you even make a formal offer, try to imagine what it would be like for you to live in the community. Start by reading the house rules: Are they compatible with your life-style? Can you live with the restrictions imposed on your use of your home? (This question is especially important if you're buying into a planned community of detached houses: It looks like you're going to be lord of your own little domain, but restrictive covenants may even limit the kind of curtains you can hang in the window!) Reading recent newsletters or board minutes can give you an idea of the issues currently affecting the community.

It's also a good idea to learn about life in the complex on a firsthand basis. If you don't know anyone who lives there, strike up a conversation with residents you meet while visiting. Try to get some sense of the interests and backgrounds of the current residents; this is especially important in small buildings where you will *have* to work closely with your neighbors. A rather bohemian lesbian couple—a music teacher and a museum administrator— moved into a Boston condo whose other residents were more conventional young couples with office jobs. The women's interests and working hours kept them from attending most building activities, so their neighbors began to assume they were snobbish and antisocial. Responding to this climate of opinion, the board began sending them formal written warnings about minor rule infractions: The chairs on their terrace, for example, were brown instead of white. The women then began to assume that their neighbors were hostile or homophobic. By this time, they had only two time-consuming alternatives: make a concerted effort to improve communication with the neighbors, or move. With a bit of advance research, they might have chosen to buy elsewhere or at least realized that they would have to make time to become active members of the community.

NEW BUILDINGS AND RECENT CONVERSIONS

Every year, the stock of shared-ownership housing grows as developers build new complexes and convert rental properties. New or just-remodeled buildings offer several advantages: new appliances, new bathrooms, building systems that meet the latest safety and performance standards, as well as the sense that this new home was prepared "just for you." There is also a substantial financial advantage: Since the developer must sell a number of homes in a relatively short time, prices may be discounted from the going market rate, bonuses like several months' free common charges may be offered; and special financing is usually available.

On the other hand, buying into a newly established condo carries special problems—problems that can last much longer than the sheen on your new refrigerator. The rest of this chapter is devoted to the particular problems of "buying new." These troubles can be physical, financial, and political.

Physical problems occur in all buildings, but new construction and conversion create their own problems. The greatest fallacy is that anything new must be in top condition. Even the most conscientious contractor makes some mistakes: Leaky roofs, defective plumbing, unreliable elevators, unpaved parking lots, and unfinished recreational facilities are common complaints among owners of newly built or renovated housing. In the case of remodelling, it's important to know what's been replaced and what potentially outdated systems were left in place. If the new refrigerator, microwave, and range are connected to inadequate wiring, you could spend more time replacing fuses than fixing dinner. And you'd have to pay dearly for rewiring.

Most developers will move to resolve the problem in a

reasonable length of time, but others may be unwilling, or even unable, to do so. A few are simply dishonest; more often, the headaches arise when a small, ambitious company underestimates the demands of a project, or when a penny-pinching developer tries to maximize profits by delaying repair expenses.

A survey conducted by the University of California at Berkeley on behalf of the California Department of Real Estate found that construction problems led nearly a quarter of all common-interest communities to plan or file law suits against the developer. In some cases, the threat of legal action or the filing of a suit prodded the developer to make an out-of-court settlement. Some of the cases had to be argued to a verdict, dragging out the process over many years and diverting the assets of both owners and developer from repairs to legal fees. The unluckiest owners could not sue because the developer had gone bankrupt.

How can a buyer avoid these headaches? First of all, don't be seduced by the fact that, at first glance, the building appears to be in good shape. If an engineer's report on the building's condition is included in the offering documents, study it closely. In the case of a rental conversion, ask if another engineer's report was prepared for the tenants negotiating committee. Ask to see the building's inspection certificate at your local buildings department. New buildings in particular are usually checked closely for adherence to safety codes.

At the same time, check out the developer's reputation. Ask your lawyer and several real estate agents (not just the one with the developer's exclusive listing!) about the company's record. Try to see a few older apartments in complexes developed by the same firm, looking closely at the quality of the workmanship and durability of the materials. Compare the quality and price of the apartment you are considering to those of competing developers; a deal "too good to be true" may be the sign of a developer who is less than ideally trustworthy. If your real estate agent declines to help you with this comparison shopping, find another. A substantial commission is factored into the sale price, and you're entitled to the professional service you're paying for.

Financial problems of new developments usually grow

from a developer's zeal to maximize the return. Holding down construction or renovation costs obviously increases profits. Low common charges can be a valuable selling point, and in buildings where the developer retains owner-ship of some rental units, keeping maintenance low helps hold down future expenses. Not surprisingly, then, some developers yield to the temptation to cut corners and set common charges so low that they cannot cover future operating expenses. Steep increases in monthly charges—totaling 30 percent, 40 percent, or more—are an all-too-frequent feature of a new condo's first five years. When poorly designed construction or inadequate modernization creates the need for major capital expenses, an additional special assessment may also be necessary.

When the developer is also the managing agent, close attention to the financial statements is required. Unit own-ers in one recently converted Brooklyn co-op were startled to receive notice that the bank holding the building's un-derlying mortgage was about to foreclose. The developer/manager had been diverting revenues from the building to other, money-losing projects, leaving the mortgage and util-ity bills unpaid. He had concealed his actions by simply failing to furnish financial statements and supporting doc-uments to the board. The consequences included several days without heat (while board members negotiated to have gas service restored), a doubling in monthly charges, and a costly, protracted legal battle, with the complete loss of all owners' equity looming as a real possibility.

The ounce of prevention here is again the developer's reputation, along with a careful examination of the build-ing's finances. Look at the figures in the offering plan closely, and have them checked by a lawyer or accountant knowledgeable in local real estate conditions. Are cost pro-jections realistic? Has a substantial reserve fund been es-tablished? If the condo has been operating for a year or more, ask to see *audited* financial statements, and ask res-ident board members how closely they monitor finances. Most developers are honest, but the few who aren't can cost you dearly.

Political problems arise from three sources: developing a working consensus among owners, establishing a relationship with renters, and managing the inevitable conflicts with the developer. When a group of people is suddenly thrown together by the accidents of the real estate market, they will need months, if not years, to get to know one another, identify leaders, and determine priorities for improvements. A buyer moving in during this early phase in a community's life has the advantage of helping to shape the development and management of the association—and the disadvantage of enduring a certain number of false starts.

The work of community building can be complicated in conversions or other developments with a substantial number of renters. It's essential to establish good communication between tenants and owners in order to head off misunderstandings that fuel resentment and hostility. If you see signs heralding division (i.e., notices of "renters only" meetings or indications that social events are open only to owners), be prepared for tension. Creative leadership can ease the problem, but it may take a considerable amount of time to establish mutual trust. One tactic that often helps is establishing a tenants council to meet regularly with the condo board. Another is involving renters in all building-wide activities. Your shared interest in making the development a pleasant place to live should help open channels of communication and cooperation.

Conflicts with the developer arise from differing perceptions of the development. The developer sees it mainly as a business investment and evaluates its financial situation in strictly bottom-line terms. For unit owners, of course, it's home, and more subjective standards apply. Unit owners, for example, are often willing to pay more for additional amenities they enjoy every day—elaborate landscaping, for example, or a higher grade of replacement window. But the sponsor, like the landlord of a rental building, would prefer to reduce costs and maximize income. In cases where the developer holds a majority of board seats, unit owners may have little control of their property; some buyers try to avoid such developments unless the rate of sale indicates that resident owners will soon gain control of the board. When the developer is managing agent, service may be good, bad, or indifferent, depending on the company's goals and organization. (See Chapter 4 for more details.)

If the sponsor holds a major share in the building you're considering, ask board members about their relationship with the sponsor to get some sense of how future disputes might affect your life in the development.

Like any form of home ownership, community associations have advantages and disadvantages. The rest of this book is dedicated to explaining how to minimize the latter and maximize the former.

2
Shared Ownership:
Understanding Your Rights and Responsibilities

In the Middle Ages, a new owner got an immediate sense of what it feels like to hold real estate. Under the formalities of what was called "Delivery of Seisin," the previous owner picked up a clod of the ground he'd just sold and plopped it into the hand of the buyer, who became—in the most literal sense—a "landholder."

Today there is nothing to exchange except a mountain of paperwork and a key. If the key is to a conventional house, you can at least dig your fingers into the backyard to get that "landholder" feeling. But if your new home is five stories up or faces a courtyard shared by a dozen neighbors, it's harder to get a grip on your new role. What's more, apartments in multiple dwellings have traditionally been the preserve of renters, so it's hard to shake the feeling that the ground, the building, and the business of running them belong to someone else. The "tenant mentality" also appeals to our all-too-human instinct for avoiding work. It's always easier to blame "them" for a problem than to face the music yourself. To make matters worse, developers tend to fill their sales brochures with idyllic images of "carefree condo living," without mentioning the financial and social tasks that unit owners must undertake in order to make a common-interest community function on a day-to-day and year-to-year basis. It's all too easy to assume that a unit owner's responsibility is no different from that of a tenant: writing a monthly check.

At the same time, though, buying a unit in a common-interest development—even a freestanding house in a planned community—does not fit conventional notions of "home ownership," either. While your freedom of choice and action are almost unlimited in traditional home ownership, in shared-interest developments you must harmonize your wishes, coordinate your plans, and, most significantly, pool your money with fellow members of the association. It's less a matter of "My home is my castle" than "Our castle is home to all of us," with a distinct set of shared-ownership rules and responsibilities, and a corresponding set of rewards and possibilities.

This chapter tries to explain what "shared ownership" means, in practical terms, for individual members and suggests ways they can take a more active—and more rewarding—role in association affairs. The specifics of group organization, finances, and management are dealt with in detail in the chapters that follow. Here are the essentials.

THE BIG PLUSES

First the good news: The entire American banking and tax system is designed to favor homeowners. If you are joining their ranks for the first time, you will be astonished by the increase in your itemized deductions, the decrease in your income tax bill, and the eagerness of bankers to lend you money. To take maximum advantage of the tax situation, be sure to change your withholding status: Working your way through the long version of the W-4 form is likely to result in a substantial increase in take-home pay or a decrease in estimated tax payments. Even if you're accustomed to doing taxes yourself, it's wise to have an accountant or other tax professional prepare your returns for your first year of ownership, to be sure you learn the proper routine and get all the advantages you're entitled to.

In addition to these immediate tax benefits, you get a long-range financial gain, as well: the equity that accumulates as you pay off your mortgage and as property values increase with inflation. Owning a unit in a condo, co-op, or planned community will not necessarily make you the next John D. Rockefeller, but it will guarantee you the opportunity to live in a home of comparable value for the indefinite future. If you're just starting a family, you can use the value built up in your unit as a financial foundation for trading up to a larger home. If you're approaching retirement, you can plan to have your mortgage substantially paid off before you retire, sharply reducing your housing costs and leaving more funds for other activities. In any case, you have a nest egg that you can live in.

Buying an apartment or town house is also an attractive option for retirees. One midwestern couple sold their suburban house for $300,000, purchased a California condo for half that sum, and banked the balance. (The tax code offers a once-in-a-lifetime break for taxpayers over fifty-five who sell their principal residences; check with your lawyer or accountant *before* striking a deal to see if you qualify.) In the process, they freed themselves from daily hassles of keeping up the house, moved to more comfortable surroundings, and increased the money available for their retirement.

As the equity builds up, you also have the option of turning it into cash with a home-equity loan—to pay for improvements, to cope with emergencies, to send the kids to college, to raise capital for any need—and at an attractive interest rate to boot. Some or all of the interest may even be tax deductible. Before you take this option, though, it's important to recall that you are, in fact, "betting the farm." Falling behind on an equity loan is just as dangerous as falling behind on the mortgage. Evaluate your future earnings potential, discuss the pros and cons with an accountant or lawyer, and weigh all the possibilities before you sign on the dotted line.

If you already own a private house, you're familiar with the financial advantages of home ownership. But you'll find some additional benefits in buying shared housing. For openers, day-to-day maintenance is no longer your sole responsibility. There's a staff to clean the gutters, shovel the snow, and repair leaky valves. You can still tend flower beds, if you wish, and you can watch someone else cut the grass while you do it. If a costly repair is needed, like modernizing the wiring, you have a group of fellow owners to share the cost—and the headaches!

Another advantage of owning your home is the freedom to decorate and adapt it to suit your needs and tastes. Structural alterations usually require board approval, but this rule is intended primarily to ensure that building systems are properly protected and that local building codes are complied with. Remodeling the bathroom, for example, should not deprive your neighbors of hot water, and moving a wall on the fifth floor should not cause the sixth, seventh, and eighth floors to sag. In applying for board approval, stress your concern for these details and show how the improvements will clearly enhance the value of your unit— and, indirectly, of the entire property. Indeed, in an older building, the board should be delighted to know that antiquated kitchens are being updated and awkward floor plans modified for today's needs. If the board refuses your request, you might apply again, making an effort to address their concerns. If you find the refusal unreasonable, you might consider the approaches to dealing with a recalcitrant board outlined on page 36.

Being an owner also means that the maintenance and service employees work for you and your neighbors—the people they see every day—and not for a landlord in some remote office. I do not recommend beginning every request for service with the line, "I pay your salary and I'm telling you . . . ," but it doesn't hurt to point out that good maintenance benefits everyone who lives and works in the complex. Developing good relationships with employees can get you not only better service but also a lot of information about how the building really works and how your maintenance fees are spent. Take a few minutes to tour the basement with the chief engineer, and you might learn whether the hot water problems are caused by an aged boiler (a big-ticket repair) or just a faulty valve (a relatively simple, inexpensive repair). Learning what happens to the trash may help you understand the rules set up by the board and the trash hauler. Watching the pool cleaners at work should explain why the pool has to be closed or drained so often.

A good working relationship does not require paying enormous tips, but the staff should be paid for work outside their usual jobs. For example, if the handyman installs your air conditioner, or if the porter disposes of an old sofa, they should be paid by you, just as you would pay an outside contractor.

THE RESPONSIBILITIES

Paying directly for jobs that might otherwise be a landlord's headache points to the key difference between renting and owning: An owner pays the bills. The rule applies not just to work in your unit, but to propertywide expenses, too: Major improvements are bound to be reflected in increased carrying charges or even a special assessment.

As a result, it pays to think twice before you make proposals to the board or at a membership meeting. If you propose an expensive project—like replacing windows, adding a swimming pool, or hiring a twenty-four-hour security guard—be prepared to discuss ways to cover the cost. (See Chapter 5, "Money Matters," for more details.) In any event, don't follow a demand for more services with a complaint about high monthly charges! It sounds incredible, but everyone who's ever served on a board has heard such an illogical series of statements from one or more unit owners.

When it comes to minor jobs, owners can save money by tending to some themselves. This might mean picking up litter dropped on the walkway, working on a gardening committee, or, in smaller buildings, replacing light bulbs in the foyer or tacking down loose carpet on the stairs.

In addition, members who have skills useful to the association can help both the group and themselves by offering those services to the building. An accountant who chairs a finance committee (or, in smaller condos, handles the books) can help fellow owners get quicker, more accurate, and less costly financial reports. A carpenter can evaluate, or even perform, key maintenance jobs. A writer can put out a newsletter.

There are limits to do-it-yourself, of course. A regular outside audit is essential, and local laws often require that certain kinds of work—plumbing and wiring, for example—be performed by a licensed specialist. Since board members are fiduciaries, responsible for the sound management of community resources, they could face serious legal consequences for failing to see that work done meets essential standards. And on a practical level, it's not very realistic to expect a volunteer committee to paint a thirty-story building, or members of a four-family co-op to completely rebuild the roof. The advantage of shared ownership is that you don't have to face these headaches alone: You can draw on the knowledge, skills, and resources of your neighbors to solve common problems. And if a major expense is involved, it's shared equitably, rather than falling on one person's sholders.

KEEPING TRACK OF YOUR MONEY

You should carefully read the financial statements that appear under your door or on your chair at an association meeting. It's not necessarily a matter of questioning the integrity or competence of board members and managers but of understanding how *your* money is spent. Pay particular attention to these points:

Regular Income and Expenses. Recurring expenses like salaries, supplies, routine maintenance, fuel and utilities, and taxes and insurance change very little from year to year and can be predicted with reasonable accuracy. Revenue is even more predictable, since the charges are set in advance. The crucial figure, of course, is the difference between expenses and revenue. If expenses match or exceed revenues, your association is in trouble, and an increase in monthly charges is imperative. If revenue considerably exceeds expenses, and you have a substantial cash reserve, it's time to talk about a reduction in fees or an increase in services. If you don't have an adequate reserve fund, it's time to start building one.

Reserve Fund. Every common-interest community needs a reserve fund sufficient to cover emergencies and seasonal variations in cash flow. In cold climates, for example, heating costs make operating expenses much higher in winter than in summer, and the reserve helps "even out" those hills and valleys. Emergencies can include both the sudden failure of a building system, like a leaking roof, or budget-busting "price shocks," like the energy crisis of the early 1970s and the skyrocketing cost of liability insurance in the middle 1980s. A reserve that is too small may force management to defer maintenance and reduce services simply to pay essential bills. In extreme cases, there is the risk of bankruptcy and the loss of everyone's equity. On the other hand, a reserve that is too large may be, literally, a waste of money; the funds might be more usefully deployed to finance capital improvements.

Auditor's Report. The annual report should be subject to an audit by a CPA; this is a requirement often imposed by the association's regulations or by state law. (Very small co-ops may have the option of being audited less frequently.) What this means, simply put, is that an outside, independent authority has checked the records and the figures to ensure that the report accurately reflects the association's financial state "in accordance with generally accepted accounting principles." If the auditor's letter includes the word *except* or any other qualifications, there are potentially serious inadequacies in the your records. Unit owners should demand immediate correction of the problem and a follow-up audit in the next quarter to ensure that future reports are accurate and complete. (For more detailed information, see "How to Read a Financial Report" in Chapter 6.) Keep in mind that the CPA certifies only the *accuracy of the numbers,* not the wisdom of the board's management. It's up to the board and individual members to interpret the figures and ask questions about any inconsistencies.

DEALING WITH AN UNCOOPERATIVE BOARD

What can an owner do when a governing board seems totally unresponsive to his or her requests, no matter how reasonably stated? Such conflicts are, alas, not uncommon, and their sources are as diverse as their solutions. Barry Willetts, for one, proposed a plan to expand the parking lot at his town house complex. Gail and Garrick Harrison wanted major repairs on the defective windows in their pre-war high-rise. And Ellen Morris wanted to see major improvements in her condo's landscaping. None of them received any response to their initial queries, forwarded through the complaint box set up by the managing agent. They each followed the same step-by-step approach, with different results:

1. *The informal fact-finding conversation.* Barry Willetts phoned the managing agent's office and spoke with the manager assigned to his complex. He discovered that local zoning laws prohibited any expansion of the parking lot; his suggestion was ignored because it was unworkable. Gail Harrison stopped the board president in the lobby and learned that window repairs were part of a large-scale rebuilding program the board was considering. Gail asked to be kept informed of progress and offered to serve on an ad hoc committee dealing with the improvements. Ellen rang the bell of a neighbor who sits on the board and asked what had happened with her proposal. The board member said they hadn't really got around to discussing it and suggested she submit a more detailed proposal for the next meeting.

As these experiences suggest, the lack of response to a request may be for a good reason, like the zoning laws or the long-term capital plan, or for a not very good reason, like "not getting around to it." The problem may even be outright incompetence or corruption, but this situation is rare. To keep the channels of communication open, then, it's always best to start by assuming that the board and managing agent are acting in good faith. An antagonistic approach is usually counterproductive, especially in the opening rounds of a dispute. It forces the people you are questioning to take a defensive stance, and what should be a search for solutions turns into a clash of egos.

In some cases, too, your antagonism may be misdirected. In relatively new developments, the most common complaints involve failures on the part of the builder or developer. A survey by the University of California at Berkeley of California condos found that nearly a quarter of the new developments had to threaten or initiate legal action against the developer. If your leaking roof, sagging floor, or unreliable elevator is the builder's fault, the board's only responsible path is to sue on behalf of the association to force the developer to make good. Meanwhile, you'll just have to live with the problem, unless you're willing to pay twice to get it solved.

2. *A formal meeting with the entire board.* Ellen Morris asked to present her landscaping ideas at a regular meeting, and the board agreed to grant her half an hour. She did some research at a local gardening center and drew up a tentative plan, complete with rough sketches and a tentative budget. While the board did not immediately accept her plan, the possibilities she suggested and the data she gathered encouraged them to move landscaping up on their agenda. In the Harrisons' building, the board decided to hold a special owners' meeting to discuss the work required on the windows and facade. The Harrisons were eager to participate, and the board put Gail in charge of an ad hoc committee to research the options.

When invited to attend a board meeting, be prepared to take advantage of the special opportunities it provides. As Ellen demonstrated, a formal presentation focuses attention on what actually can or should be done, and it helps to shift attention from personality differences to substantive issues. Be ready to follow up, as both Gail and Ellen clearly were.

At the same time, it's important to remain flexible and to look for areas of compromise acceptable to you. The management of Hill Crest Towers had to knock a hole in Mrs. Simmons' living room wall to complete a rewiring project. Fearing that a patch would be glaringly conspicuous, she asked the board to repaint the entire room. But the development had a long-standing policy of repainting only the damaged area. "We can't afford to include a complete redecorating job in every repair project," the board president explained. As long as both sides remained adamant, nothing happened, and Mrs. Simmons was left with a hole in the wall. Finally Mrs. Simmons' son offered to buy the paint if the association would paint the entire wall—a much less conspicuous repair than just painting the patch. The Board accepted this offer, and the work was finally completed, pleasing everyone.

3. *Raise the issue at the annual general meeting.* This is a good way to demonstrate or discover how widely an issue affects unit owners in the complex as a whole. Ellen asked about the landscaping plans and found that other unit owners were concerned about the shabby condition of the grounds. As a result, the board promised to allocate funds for the next planting season. Gail Harrison had a different experience: When the question of facade repairs came up, she was startled to hear the long list of complaints that her neighbors voiced. She decided that her committee would have to draw up a comprehensive list of problems, so that as many of them as possible could be addressed in the improvement work. While the chance to solve so many problems in one project was welcome, the delays and added expense involved became the source of complaints in their own right. Barry brought up the parking issue at his annual meeting, hoping to hear some new ideas for solving the problem. But all that developed was a shouting match between two unit owners who accused each other of flouting parking rules.

These experiences highlight the advantages and disadvantages of discussing improvements in the large-scale context of an annual meeting. It's an efficient way to get a broad-scale sense of the owners' feelings, but it's not an especially good forum for working out details. Gail, for example, learned how large a task she'd taken on, but needed to follow up later. Barry would have gotten farther if he had offered one or more specific proposals for discussion rather than opening the door to a wide-ranging—and easily sidetracked—discussion.

4. *When negotiations fail.* It's always quicker and less costly to solve problems through negotiation and compromise, but sometimes this approach doesn't work. The managing agent may be incompetent. The board may be complacent, careless, or simply insensitive to the needs of unit owners. In such circumstances, there are two avenues of redress: You can take legal action against the association or you can organize a campaign to replace all or most board members.

Legal action can be undertaken at any time and brings the great satisfaction of naming an official winner. But legal precedents are on the side of the association unless you can prove fraud or theft, so there is a good chance you will lose the case, as well as a lot of money and goodwill. A man in a Cincinnati town house development, for example, refused to paint his front door and windows in the uniform color the board had selected, even though the condo's governing documents clearly gave the association the right to control the appearance of the facade. After protracted legal action, carried all the way to the state's highest court, he was told that the governing documents were legal and enforceable. He had to repaint the door and pay a hefty legal bill as well. Furthermore, he had to pay a portion of the association's legal expenses, too; they were factored into his (and every other owner's) common charges.

A more effective and less costly way to change board policies is to replace the board members. Talk to your neighbors to discover if other unit owners have unresolved complaints and desire a change. If so, an effort to organize an insurgent slate to run in the next board elections may well bear fruit. Indeed, a board that overlooks the owners' interests is one that *needs* to be replaced. This approach does require waiting for the next annual meeting—and possibly for the one after that, too, if your board has staggered terms—but it can bring definitive change in the direction you want to go.

To begin an insurgent campaign, organize a meeting of people most eager to bring about change. You can announce the meeting through word of mouth, depending on personal contacts and their contacts to reach interested parties, or you can post a formal notice. Once you have candidates and a platform, you're ready to start drumming up support among your neighbors. If the complex is large, you will probably want to do some formal campaigning, including posters on bulletin boards, flyers circulated in mailboxes or under doors, and handshaking by entrances to the complex. In smaller developments, a less formal approach should work: a few flyers slipped under doors, conversations around the swimming pool or in the laundry room, and a reminder poster as the election approaches. If there are absentee owners who sublet the apartments they own, get their addresses from the managing agent and mail them a letter and flyers. Try to keep your campaign literature focused on specific issues rather than personalities. Even if you cannot gain a majority of the board in one election, demonstrating broad support for your concerns can force the board to deal with them.

Sometimes this type of concerted campaign will win a victory even before the formal elections, when incumbents choose to withdraw and leave the burdens of running the association to more eager candidates. If the decision comes down to a contested election, be sure that you understand the voting rules laid down in your governing documents. At the election, be sure these rules are followed and that votes are properly tallied. You may want to ask the condo's lawyer to attend the meeting to advise both sides on questions of procedure. After the elections, be sure all ballots and other papers are preserved to settle any disputes that may arise.

Win or lose, you can take credit for increasing owner participation and reminding both the board and the managing agent of who is really in charge.

ANSWERS TO YOUR QUESTIONS

If you have any questions about how your development is run, or if you are planning work or making a request to the board, start first with the governing documents. From such mundane issues as where to walk your dog to key questions about electing directors, these documents lay down the rules and regulations governing key aspects of community life. Some legalisms may be obscure, but most of the points are spelled out in clear, everyday language. (See Chapter 6 for more details.) If the regulations make painting the unit your responsibility, there's no point in asking the board to do it for you. If you think board members should serve staggered terms to enhance continuity, you'll have to prepare an amendment to the by-laws for discussion at the next association meeting. If you'd like to change guest regulations for the health club, you'll have to follow the procedures for amending the house rules. Knowing why a rule began and who has the power to change it—or why a change is not practical—can save you a lot of wasted energy.

Even more important, cooperation among owners, and between individual owners and the board, goes more smoothly when everyone knows the ground rules. It's a rare association meeting in which someone doesn't tell another owner, with considerable exasperation, "If you'd read your prospectus, you wouldn't even ask!" Ignorance, in this case, breeds strife, while a preparatory glance at the appropriate papers could lay the groundwork for compromise and agreement.

FINDING YOUR NICHE

"These formalities are all very well," I hear you say, "but what can *I* do for the association? I'm not a lawyer or a CPA; plants die when I touch them; and I can't tell one end of a hammer from another. Am I just a fifth wheel?" The answer is simply, "Keep your eyes open." In one four-family co-op, an habitual early riser and a "night person" struck up a partnership to regulate the heat: The unit owner accustomed to going to bed at midnight or 1:00 AM turns down the thermostat (conveniently located in a hallway), while the teacher who rises at 5:45 turns it up. (Unlike a "setback" thermostat, this system requires no rewiring and automatically adjusts for weekends and holidays.) A young couple moving into a ninety-six-unit building didn't think of themselves as "joiners." But when neighbors heard the husband playing the piano, they asked him to give lessons to their children, and the apartment became a gathering place for the building's music lovers.

The needs of a bona fide community are not all pragmatic matters of maintenance and accounting. Symbols of shared interest and involvement are very important. If you have some homemade seasonal decorations, like children's Thanksgiving drawings, why not put them up in the foyer? If your unit is near the mailboxes, why not offer to maintain a bulletin board? Sometimes your own frustrations can suggest ways to make living in the development more pleasant. A young executive, purchasing her first home and moving to a new city, found herself researching local merchants and services. A few months later, she realized that her notes could serve as the core of a neighborhood guide, and, with some help from other residents, she produced a comprehensive handbook for the association.

The most important activities are the ones that give neighbors an occasion to get to know one another, exchange views, and catch up on local news. If you enjoy organizing parties, why not plan something for the condo? A tree-trimming party at Christmas and a summer barbecue in the yard are proven successes. If you live in a very large development, it would be useful to establish mechanisms for communicating between individual sections and the development as a whole; you could organize floor committees, social committees, or similar groups. How about a parents' club to share experiences and trade baby-sitting chores? Or a drama club for teens? Start with small meetings in your unit and move to larger quarters—on-site or in nearby facilities, like churches or schools—as attendance grows. In planning any event, take the nature and interests of all members into account: games for kids, for example, a sing-along led by the professional singer in 5C, or lessons in creating origami ornaments to get lots of folks involved during the holidays.

Many of these suggestions seem obvious, but it's always a mistake to assume that they will, in some way, just happen. Even the best idea takes follow-up and persistence, especially in relatively new condos. In one such development, the gardening committee chair found herself dragging her daughter, three board members, and their spouses into the courtyard for the first spring's seasonal plantings. As the gardens took shape, though, more volunteers came out, and after three years a core of four active gardeners gave the grounds a handsome look year-round. The most insidious myth about these groups is that the board will organize them. If your association is well established, the board may have rejected such a role for itself. On the other hand, you may have an idea that had never occurred to a board member. If your condo was started only recently, board members are probably preoccupied with figuring out the best management strategy, discovering reliable contractors, and educating themselves about the development's needs and possibilities. It's advisable to discuss your ideas with the board, which is likely to welcome any constructive offer. You'll need official board approval to take on a formal role responsibility, like Chair of the Finance Committee, but nothing more than an informal blessing is required for initiatives like holiday parties. It's your home and your money, so don't be afraid to add your own touch.

Finally, there is one way any member can help the entire association: running for the board. You may not think of yourself as a take-charge type, but the board has many responsibilities (see Chapter 3) and needs many talents. More significantly, it also needs the involvement of as many residents as possible. The concerns and interests of those who are reluctant to serve are sometimes ignored, simply because there is no one to voice them. Also, if authority is concentrated in the hands of a few, the small but very real possibility of corruption and mismanagement arises.

In one co-op, where shareholders complacently elected the same board over and over again, a new purchaser inspected the financial report and discovered that the constant increases in maintenance charges were not adequately accounted for. In fact, research showed they were going largely to purchase new cars and overseas vacations for board members. A costly court battle ensued, and even greater hikes in maintenance fees were needed to cover the repairs that had been deferred by the profiteers. When it comes to your money, ignorance is not bliss, and the best way to learn how it is spent is to serve on the board.

3
The Board:
Making Shared Ownership Work

"The Board of Managers shall have full responsibility for the day-to-day operations of the Association." In words such as these, the charter of the typical association thrusts broad and complex responsibilities on a small number of willing but often inexperienced members. At the same time, it creates the impression in some residents that these men and women have become honorary landlords, if not minor deities, able to re-sod a lawn at the snap of a finger or re-build an elevator at the wave of a hand. In this chapter, I'll try to dispel the myths by explaining how an effective board runs and what it actually does.

WHO IS A CANDIDATE FOR MEMBERSHIP?

Ideally, every unit owner should serve a few terms on the board, so that every member of the community can have firsthand knowledge of its organization and operations; it can be an invaluable, eye-opening experience. Of course, this self-education requires a certain investment of time. Regular monthly meetings take two or three hours, but this is just the beginning of the time required. Follow-up work on specific projects, ad hoc discussions with other board members, and meetings with building employees and committee members can take another two or three hours a week. If a major change is in the works—replacing the roof, large-scale renovations, hiring a new managing agent—even more time will be required.

Given the time and willingness to serve, what other qualifications should a board member have? Experience in real estate management would be ideal, but it's rare. I do, however, know a Brooklyn woman who parlayed her experience on a co-op board into a successful career in real estate management! Lawyers, accountants, carpenters, plumbers, gardeners, writers, and office managers all bring obvious qualifications to the job, but such specific credentials aren't really necessary. Anyone with reasonable intelligence, common sense, and a desire to learn can quickly pick up the essentials.

Far more important are the personal qualities: patience, persistence, and a sense of humor. You don't want to make important spending commitments without patiently considering all the options. You'll need patient forbearance to cope with the inevitable conflicts among unit owners, managers, and employees. You won't get any significant projects completed without persistent follow-up, and when the color that looked great on the paint chip looks lousy on the door, you must be able to laugh, especially at yourself.

Who should *not* run? There are two types of potential candidates who might find running for or serving on the board a major disappointment. The first is the bluntly outspoken person whose candor might be mistaken for hostility by other unit owners. In one New York condo, for example, a professional woman who always came to association meetings with a series of important but often needling questions for the board announced her own candidacy and finished dead last in the elections. Many of her fellow owners apparently feared that she would be difficult to deal with in a position of authority.

Another type of candidate headed for frustration is the "single-issue" candidate. A determination to replace the decrepit, aging windows is a worthy goal, but if the leaky roof and brickwork must be repaired first, you may not be able to attain it in one or two terms. Each board member must be willing to reconsider his or her priorities in terms of the needs and the resources of the development as a whole.

Briefly put, everyone should run for the board who is curious about the operations of the association, tolerant of human foibles, and willing to work seriously at making life more pleasant for themselves and their neighbors.

GETTING ORGANIZED

The regulations specify the number of board members: Five, seven, or nine is typical, to keep the size manageable and avoid tie votes. The regulations also specify officers: a president, vice-president, secretary, and treasurer, usually selected by the board from among its members. Naming officers is more important in dealing with others than in the board's internal operations, so newly elected board members can safely postpone the decision for a couple of weeks while they take the time to get to know one another.

Setting Up a Framework

When it comes to organization, a few purely mechanical steps will work wonders in smoothing out operations. First of all, decide on a regular day for your formal board meeting (e.g., the third Wednesday of each month) and *stick to this schedule*. A sense of inevitability, no matter how artificial, will keep everyone working to meet the deadline. Second, designate an individual (president, secretary, or site manager) to draw up a working agenda, which can be as simple as a list of complaints received and projects in progress. Third, begin every monthly meeting with the financial report. Money is the ultimate constraint on all your actions, and the financial report is the place where future problems first become apparent. Make sure your meeting is scheduled late enough in the month to have the previous month's report on hand. If your bookkeeper or managing agent can't deliver the numbers in time, find another!

When terms are staggered, or if some members have

been reelected, the board will consist of both new and returning members. This situation places extra responsibilities on the "old" members. They must make a special effort to involve the newcomers, even if it takes the point-blank query, "Mary, what do you think we should do?" or "Jack, will you please follow up on this tomorrow?" They might also consider trading some of their tasks or titles in order to take advantage of the interests and talents of newly elected members. Especially in small condos—where the same unit owners *must* serve on the board year after year— rotating tasks among the board members is a good way to maintain interest.

Delegating Responsibilities

After laying the groundwork for internal cooperation, members should direct attention to their relations with the outside world. It is at this point that a certain degree of formality becomes inevitable. Banks, brokers, managing agents, contractors, and creditors all want to know who is "in charge." Even the smallest co-op benefits from an understanding that one specific person is responsible for financial affairs, another is responsible for the garden and grounds, and a third is responsible for an ongoing project, like repaving the driveway or installing a pool heater.

Electing four officers from a body of five or even seven members may appear to be a purely arbitrary exercise, but grounds for a sound choice are often easy to find. One board, for example, had a member who was a public relations professional; she became president, since that officer is the one expected to represent the co-op on formal occasions and deal with requests for information. The computer buff was elected treasurer, since he could easily track building finances with his spreadsheet program. The lawyer on the board was named secretary, since that's the position responsible for paperwork and government relations. A freelance writer was named vice-president, since he was willing to edit a newsletter and handle communications tasks.

Not all boards possess such a convenient array of professional backgrounds, but a close look at each member's talents and interests will usually turn up a likely candidate for each job. The person with a head for figures, whose checkbook always balances, is clearly destined to be treasurer. The member who takes the most detailed notes at the first few meetings would make a good secretary. And the member who keeps bringing the conversation back to the most important points? Sounds like a president to me. If you want to demonstrate that everyone on the board has an important responsibility, you can also create specific titles for nonofficers: Chair of the Audit Committee, Supervisor of Employee Relations, Communications Director, etc.

Advisory Committees

There's no reason to make the association a one- (or five- or seven-) person band. If any residents are eager to help but intimidated by the scope of board responsibilities, try to get them on a working committee. A grounds committee, a newsletter committee, and a recreation committee are common fixtures in co-ops and condos. When a particular project is involved—landscaping the grounds, redecorating the public areas, or improving the lighting, to cite three common examples—an ad hoc committee can be established.

If your association doesn't have any advisory committees, consider starting one or more at your next unit owners meeting. The technique is simple. If Mary Smith makes provocative suggestions for better sharing of the pool between children and adults, ask her to chair a new pool committee. But don't leave her holding the bag. Immediately ask for volunteers to help her survey owners' opinions, put up signs, and evaluate the new rules. Encourage anyone who seems uncertain to speak up. And make sure Mary gets all the names, addresses, and phone numbers of her volunteer committee members. If Bill Black asks probing questions about the financial report, ask him to chair an audit committee—and make sure he gets help, too.

These examples suggest some basic rules: First, each committee must correspond to the interests of its members. If no one has a green thumb, don't try to organize a gardening committee; you'll have to rely on your staff or an out-side contractor to maintain the grounds. Second, and equally important, each committee's responsibilities and rewards should be clearly defined. If the goal is redecorat-ing the lobby, set up a step-by-step schedule—researching alternatives, seeking out the best prices, making the pur-chase decisions, supervising the installation—and make sure the people who did the work get thanked in public when the job is finished. Third, no matter what the com-mittee's goal, be sure to schedule regular follow-up meet-ings between the committee chair and the board to keep the project on track. If problems arise, the board should not hesitate to intervene, diplomatically but decisively. It may be necessary to work out a new schedule, involve more unit owners on the committee, or take on part of the job your-selves.

Ground Rules for Effective Decision Making

The first priorities of a newly elected board should be build-ing a sense of shared responsibility and encouraging the habit of decision by consensus. In one interracial co-op, for example, the board split into a black group and a white group, each side scarcely speaking to the other. As a result, no action could be taken for an entire year. Even when such conspicuous potential divisions do not exist, matters of per-sonality and style can become divisive factors. To develop mutual trust and understanding, it's a good idea to start a new term by working on issues on which agreement comes easily. If the halls look shoddy, for example, make redeco-rating public areas your first priority. If there's a great view from your upper floors, adding a roof deck might be a good place to start. If interest rates are falling, a co-op might consider refinancing the building mortgage; in fact, that's how the biracial co-op's new board got things restarted.

Where there is strong disagreement, try to avoid emo-tional reactions and listen closely to what others are saying, looking for potential areas of compromise. A member who has not yet taken a strong position can often take the lead in seeking out areas of agreement. Don't hesitate to postpone a particularly difficult decision. All board members should want to do what's best for the development and should recognize that they must eventually forge an agreement. With some time to reflect on opposing points of view, encouraged by pressure from fellow owners and, perhaps, an imminent deadline, they'll often find some way to compromise.

For example, the board of a suburban condo paid a landscape architect to prepare elaborate plans to redesign the grounds. Bids from contractors were more than double preliminary estimates, forcing the board to rethink the entire project. One member pressed for completing the work as designed, despite the cost, because of the design's great appeal. Another argued for postponing the garden work indefinitely and using the funds to redecorate the building's public areas. A third member offered to discuss cost-saving modifications with the architect, but he was unable to make any significant reductions. By this time, the planting season had passed, and the matter was put aside. The following spring, the board, eager to improve the appearance of the building, took another look at the original plan and agreed to adapt it to the limited budget. The scaled-down version— the same trees and shrubs, without the custom-made planters and paved walkways—was quickly completed, and the azaleas were blooming by Easter. If either side had pressed for an immediate yes-or-no vote when the initial bids came in, the entire project might have been killed. By waiting and reconsidering, each side achieved its most important goal: a balanced budget and a spruced-up yard.

Inevitably, there will be a few points on which a consensus is impossible to reach. But once a climate of mutual respect and cooperation has been developed, the search for a workable compromise becomes easier. The more deepseated the differences, though, the more time and trouble it will take to resolve them. A Philadelphia condo board, for example, could not agree on whether or not to maintain twenty-four-hour doorman service. While doormen were a convenience to residents and a boost for security, their salaries and fringe benefits were the fastest-growing items in a budget squeezed by rising costs all around. The matter was debated for more than two years before it became clear that a majority of the board favored elimination of the doormen, as long as steps were taken to compensate for their absence—steps such as installing electronic security devices and arranging to have a porter on call to assist residents with luggage and packages. The minority, satisfied that the board had tried to accommodate them within the limits of the budget, "agreed to disagree," with the clear understanding that the issue would be reopened if there were any evidence that this reduction in services was compromising building security or reducing the resale value of owners' apartments.

LEADERSHIP RESPONSIBILITIES

The board is ultimately responsible for establishing policies and priorities for the association as a whole. But you can't be a leader unless the other unit owners agree to follow. And the best way to accomplish that is the same patient consensus building that makes the board itself work effectively. Here's a case history of consensus building, applied to a common and contentious issue: what to do about deteriorated windows.

The Colonial was built in the 1930s in a Georgian style, with twelve-pane double-hung windows. The years had taken their toll, and many windows were loose, damaged, or totally inoperable. One group of unit owners wanted to replace them with modern aluminum windows, which would be easier to care for: They never require painting, can be tilted inward for easy cleaning, and provide better insulation against both the cold and the noise of the street. Another group insisted on nothing but wood replacement windows, to preserve the building's character. Since the Colonial stood in a historic district, the windows' appearance was a matter of law as well as aesthetics.

The board interviewed contractors experienced in both kinds of renovation and found itself unable to come to a clear decision. The wood windows were more attractive but much more expensive, especially after factoring in additional costs like painting and storm windows. The metal windows fit the budget much better and promised a lot of convenience, but since they were relatively new to the market, their long-term durability had never been tested in day-to-day use. Many of the designs proposed were clearly inappropriate for the building, and no metal windows could be installed without a special permit from the Landmarks Commission. To make the decision even more difficult, there was no accurate assessment of the windows' current condition, or even a count of how many windows the building had!

In search of some solid, useful information, the board turned to a consulting architect, who organized a comprehensive window survey. His study highlighted previously underestimated problems with the roof and suggested a third alternative for the windows: rehabilitating the present windows, including replacement of those elements that were clearly beyond repair. With this information in hand, the board was able to transform a subjective debate into a straightforward matter of dollars and cents. At the same time, impatience with the old windows was driving the two opposing sides toward consensus. The "preservationists" were forced to admit that wooden replacement windows would be too expensive, especially with major roof repairs added to the budget. And the "pragmatists" agreed to accept the rehabilitation option, provided it proved economically comparable to metal replacement windows. By the time the board reached its final decision, it was widely supported by the unit owners, who were convinced that the option chosen was the best allocation of the co-op's limited resources.

Making and Enforcing Rules

The board's leadership responsibilities include not only setting priorities for finance and maintenance but also establishing and enforcing rules and regulations for the community as a whole. It's worth the time to sit down and study the current house rules. If some rules are not being observed—let alone enforced—they should be repealed. If a third of the unit owners keep pets, for example, it's time to remove the "no pets" rule. Trying to enforce an unrealistic rule can only create resentment and, if pressed to its legal extreme, could lead to a court nullifying the rule on the grounds that the board had abdicated its right to enforce it. If the board, however, announces a revision of the rules to make them coincide with the way members of the association actually live, it will produce two results: first, it will demonstrate an awareness of members' interests and lifestyles, and second, it will redirect attention to the rules and their importance.

Sometimes it's difficult to determine what sort of rules meet residents' expectations. A California planned community had rules prohibiting owners from pruning trees or shrubs; a firm of professional forestry experts had been hired to maintain the "natural woodland" look that was a key selling point of the community. But the board found itself plagued by "midnight clippers"—unit owners who surreptitiously sawed off low-hanging branches because they preferred spectacular views from their windows to a "natural look" to the grounds. Pleas in the community newsletter failed to stop the unauthorized cutting, and the board was unable to determine who was responsible. It took an acrimonious meeting and a redefinition of landscaping goals to make the no-pruning rule acceptable and enforceable.

If the rules are reasonable and livable, then it's important to enforce them, diplomatically but firmly. One condo, for example, had a recurring problem with a unit owner who persisted in walking his dog in the building's interior courtyard. Many residents were afraid of the dog—a large German Shepherd—and the gardening committee was understandably irritated by the damage the pet had done to their flowers. A notice in the newsletter reiterating the no-dogs-in-the-courtyard rule and a verbal reminder to the person involved produced no results, so the board asked its lawyer to write a warning letter. By indicating the degree of seriousness with which the board viewed the issue, this letter got results, and the problem disappeared. If warnings don't work, the board should discuss the next step with the condo's lawyers. Your development's charter, as well as local housing law, will spell out the remedies available, but persistent violations of house rules are usually ranked with failure to pay monthly carrying charges in degree of seriousness, and a declaration of default could be the final step.

While enforcing rules, it's important not to overlook building employees. If your planned community has a strict no-parking-in-the-streets rule, don't let your groundskeepers leave a jumble of pickups and mowers in front of the maintenance building. If unit owners are required to place their refuse in specific containers, the resident manager's garbage should not be piled up alongside in a cardboard box.

Mediating Disputes

Noisy parties, clashing musical tastes, sloppy housekeeping, rambunctious children—disputes among residents spring up for any number of reasons, but the board is usually the first place they turn to resolve them. Sometimes, the problem is specifically addressed in the house rules. If several residents heard a loud party at 2:00 AM, and the house rules specify that loud music is not to be played after 11:00 PM, then the infraction is clear. Sometimes, however, the matter is more ambiguous, and the board's role may be more difficult. When an irate neighbor rings your bell berating "those inconsiderate slobs" or "that ill-mannered brat," here are some guidelines that will serve you (and your neighbors) well:

1. *Define the problem.* Pay close attention and ask questions to determine what, precisely, happened. There may simply be a clash of personalities, or there may be clear matters of fact that determine who is at fault and what remedies are required.

2. *Don't promise anything except your attention.* Listen sympathetically and understand the person's need to let off steam, but be careful to avoid prejudging the issues or making promises you may not be able to keep.

3. *Get all the facts.* Discuss the problem with the other party in the dispute. If there is a question of fact (e.g., has a fence been installed contrary to community rules? is an owner using her unit to conduct business, contrary to local

law?), the board should organize a formal inspection visit and report to both parties.

4. *Discuss the issues.* Talk informally with fellow board members to get a sense of how they see the dispute. If the issues are ambiguous, look for points the two sides have in common or other grounds for compromise.

5. *Recognize that there may be nothing you can do except express concern and encourage the two sides to talk.* If, for example, the "noisy" neighbors have installed extra carpet, bought earphones for the stereo, and rearranged their daily schedules, they've already done everything you could reasonably ask. All you can do is remind the complainer that hearing the neighbors is part of apartment living, then make a plea for patience and tolerance.

6. *Above all, keep yourself out of the argument.* Your success as a mediator—and as an administrator of the association—depends on your being perceived as fair, even-handed, and willing to consider the needs of all residents. As soon as you take sides, you risk losing your credibility, and every part of your job gets much harder.

The site manager—particularly one whose office is part of the development itself—can also serve this mediating function. Larger complexes sometimes establish a "resident relations" committee to deal with it. (See the description of "Advisory Committees," page 49.) The same rules apply, and the Board should be prepared to step in promptly if the "first-line" mediator's efforts fail to resolve or calm the dispute.

The Recalcitrant Owner

It happens in every association: One unit owner always pays late, skips membership meetings, ignores pleas for help or, in extreme cases, has unauthorized work done in the unit or tries to sell without notice. Such a person is always costly and annoying; in a small building, the situation may be disastrous. What can a board do?

The board has some powerful legal weapons—including, ultimately, foreclosure and eviction—but using these weapons costs a great deal of money, time, and energy. Before reaching for The Bomb, therefore, it's worth trying a more gradual approach. First, arrange a face-to-face meeting and explain how the offender is hurting the development by ignoring the rules. Be calm and rational; avoid name-calling or other emotional accusations. There may be an honest misunderstanding. The owner may view the problem as a recalcitrant board and may be considering legal action on his or her own—another good reason to try to understand the owner's point of view and seek a face-to-face settlement.

If, within a month, you don't see signs of improvement or reconciliation, ask your lawyer to write a formal warning letter to the offending owner, detailing the rule infractions and outlining the risks of noncompliance. The involvement of an outside party emphasizes the seriousness of the situation and moves the dispute onto a formal plane. Follow up the letter with another face-to-face meeting and try again for a resolution.

If all else fails, you can declare the owner in default and start legal action. The first step is to notify the bank holding the defaulter's mortgage, an action which gets a powerful ally on the association's side. Since the owner's default could imperil the bank's collateral, the bank has a strong interest in "curing" the default as quickly as possible. Default is appealingly definitive, but it has a distinctly "lose-lose" effect. If the owner remedies the situation under legal pressure, you've got yourself an angry and resentful neighbor. If the owner can't meet his obligations, he'll probably be forced into bankruptcy, and you'll have a unit tied up in litigation for months, producing no revenue to pay the association's bills, which will, of course, grow larger, thanks to legal expenses. Like The Bomb, default is a weapon to be used only as a last resort.

One final rule in dealing with a recalcitrant owner: Act quickly. If unauthorized renovations are involved, for example, it's much easier to stop work that's just begun than to undo completed alterations or repair damage caused by bad planning. If missed monthly payments are the problem, it will only get worse with time. One condo board, trying to be patient with a troubled neighbor, waited five months before taking action against a nonpayer. It found itself in line behind the IRS and the owner's bank in an involuntary bankruptcy action. Remember that board members are responsible for protecting the interests of *all* owners and couid be liable to legal action themselves for failing to act promptly when the association's financial interests are at stake.

SOCIAL AND COMMUNICATIONS RESPONSIBILITIES: MAKING THE COMMUNITY WORK

In addition to providing leadership in matters of formal policy, the board should try to create a feeling of community among the owners, both to make life more pleasant and to enhance the awareness that all share responsibility for the development. Keeping owners informed about conditions affecting their shared investment, spiking unfounded rumors, and maintaining good relations among neighbors are three goals that can be approached with strategies like the following.

Greeting Newcomers

A sense of community starts with recognizing names and faces, and the sooner the better for people who have just moved into the complex. Newcomers naturally feel a bit disoriented and welcome the chance to get to know more about their new neighbors, and there are various strategies for meeting this need. When a screening interview is required, it automatically gives new owners the chance to meet the board; this interview can also serve as an orientation session. Where no interview is required, the board can establish the custom of a voluntary "welcome interview" with new owners at the time they move in. In some cases the initiative for a meeting may come from a buyer seeking answers to questions he or she may have about the condo and its policies. Larger developments sometimes establish welcoming committees to visit new residents as soon as they move in or even ask a member of the management staff to take on this responsibility. Very small condos can handle the task informally, with each neighbor stopping by the newcomer's home whenever convenient.

However the meeting is arranged and whoever conducts it, board members should ask about the newcomers' special interests, suggest ways these interests might be useful to the association, and mention any upcoming events you've planned. Whether the meeting is formal or informal, be sure to ask if the newcomer has any questions; if you can't provide the answer on the spot, be sure to explain who does have the answer. If you have a resident's handbook (see page 173), this is the time to deliver it. If the residents of adjacent units are at home, ring their bells and make the appropriate introductions. When you encounter the newcomer and another owner in the mail room, the laundry, or the health club, don't hesitate to ask, "Have you met Barry Brown, the new owner of 7H?" And take the time at the beginning of each meeting to let the members introduce themselves.

Meetings

In most states, business laws require that at least one general membership meeting be held each year; some boards prefer to hold additional meetings to keep members abreast of developments in the association. But the results of any meeting depend primarily on how well the board has planned and prepared for the meeting. An all-too-familiar pattern is a loosely run session beginning with a brief report from each board member, followed by highly vocal complaints from a handful of residents. The *New York Times* reports that members of an Atlanta condo once devoted forty minutes to haggling over the temperature of the swimming pool. Resolving complaints is indeed part of the board's job, and board members must expect to receive criticism, both justified and eccentric. But there's no reason why a meeting to serve all unit owners should get hijacked by a few complainers.

The best way to avoid this problem is to prepare a formal report for the annual meeting, summarizing actions taken and outlining a program for the coming year. Be sure to include financial details and explain major money matters such as increases in the maintenance charge or major projects to be undertaken. Make the items in the annual report the main points of the agenda, with questions to follow *later*. This procedure ensures that associationwide issues get primary attention and that individual complaints are brought up largely in the context of broader, underlying problems. The fact that the evening is likely to be a long one also focuses attention on the most urgent complaints: Hunger and fatigue discourage frivolous arguments.

While it's important to control the agenda, this does not mean discouraging participation from members. Begin the evening with a round of self-introductions by all present to foster a neighborly atmosphere. If a good question is raised at a bad time, the presiding officer should take a note of it and make a point of returning to the questioner when the appropriate point is reached in the agenda. For example, during the discussion of the window-rebuilding project, Mrs. Gomez asks if the heating system can be better adjusted. Rather than allow the discussion to get sidetracked, the presiding officer should promise to call on Mrs. Gomez when the heating item on the agenda is reached. If a particularly insistent owner keeps pressing a personal complaint, politely explain that further discussion in front of the whole group would be pointless and set a date and time for appropriate follow-up, such as an inspection by the board.

If your building is small or if board members prefer face-to-face communications, you may wish to hold frequent meetings of the entire membership. Alternatively, you might hold regular board meetings on an "open" basis, with unit owners invited to observe or comment. In fact, some states require that board meetings be open to all association members. But even if the meeting is small, a well-planned, focused agenda will help everyone make more effective use of the time.

A good agenda can also help you decide whether to invite any guests. Your accountant might come to discuss your financial plans, an engineer to discuss the reconstruction of the roof, or the condo's lawyer to resolve questions about individual residents' privileges. In fact, some boards invite these professionals to all membership meetings as a matter of course. Keep in mind, however, that these folks charge their regular fees for attending such meetings, and you might prefer to save this money if there are no urgent matters on the agenda. Specific queries can often be handled more efficiently by a brief phone call during business hours.

Newsletter

Except in very small co-ops, where all the owners see one another almost every day, a regularly circulated periodical (every month or every other month) is the most efficient way to communicate with all residents. In addition to news of board decisions, reminders of association policies, and notices about the impact of work schedules or holidays on building services, the newsletter can be enhanced with news of community affairs—a library bake sale, a church social, a house tour, reviews of new shops and restaurants, and any personal touches the editor can bring to it. The newsletter can also be a tool for putting residents in touch with one another. A want-ad section, for example, can let neighbors know who is good at needlecrafts, who needs a dog-walker, who runs a local catering business, who needs a French language tutor, and who's available for baby-sitting. One "department" is essential, however: The newsletter must explain where to send comments on the paper, where to direct complaints, and who is responsible for each of the activities described. As far as possible, it should be a forum for two-way communication.

In medium-sized developments, one of the board members can serve as newsletter editor-publisher, taking responsibility for writing, duplicating, and distributing it. In larger complexes, several residents can be involved in a newsletter committee, and distribution can be handled by the management staff. In the interests of broader participation, the editor need not be a member of the board, but at least one member of the board should work closely with the editor to make sure policy is communicated unambiguously. See page 171 for a sample newsletter.

Parties and/or Work Groups

Contrary to the old saying, business and pleasure can be mixed in running a shared-interest development. One of the best ways to strengthen your community is to organize an occasion where members have the chance to get together, drink a bit of soda or wine, and enjoy conversation. Purely social events, like a poolside barbecue, can provide a time and a place to open channels of communication in a relaxed environment. "Work" and play can be combined in events like a tree-trimming party, where residents join together to fold origami ornaments, string popcorn and cranberries, or festoon the lobby with store-bought decorations. Even such dreary tasks as painting the stairwell take on a festive air when all the people who live there join together to do the work.

If some of your building's residents are renters—either tenants who have remained in residence since before the conversion or those who have rented from investors—it's a good idea to involve them in these buildingwide activities. Common sense suggests, and a statewide survey in California confirms, that renters who feel they are part of the community are much more willing to abide by house rules and cooperate with the board and manager.

Special Events

Keep an eye out for noteworthy talents or achievements among your neighbors. Your resident musicians might give a recital in the lobby or recreation room. The student who won a prize in a local science fair could give a presentation at a special supper. A resident stage director or playwright could arrange a one-of-a-kind experience for the holiday season. Encourage suggestions and let your imagination run wild!

A Handbook

A handy reference for all owners, and an excellent complement to your meetings with newcomers, this is a summary of association policies and facilities, updated and circulated regularly. The handbook should explain key parts of the house rules and governing charter, especially such potentially contentious questions as pets, noise, and repairs. The last point is particularly important, since owners are often confused about which repairs are the board's responsibility and which must be taken care of by the individual. If association employees are available to do work for individual owners, be sure to spell out the conditions that apply. (For more information on repairs, see "Maintenance Responsibilities," page 67.)

Don't overlook other practical matters, either: swimming pool hours, assignment of parking spaces, rules for using the service elevator, etc. This type of information is especially important in resort areas, where residents often have houseguests. You may even want to produce a concise summary of the rules just for guests. If you're ambitious or have several contributors, you can also add a local shopping directory to help newcomers find the goods and services they need. The more useful and engaging the handbook, the more closely it will be read.

Goodwill and the Bottom Line

Does it really matter whether people in your development get along? Sure, it's a bit nicer, but what does it have to do with money? First of all, those work groups can save a lot of maintenance expenses. But more important, a cooperative spirit can also forestall legal problems. One condo lawyer, for example, after spending the previous year filing and defending court actions brought by shareholders against the board and by the board against shareholders, made a blunt observation when she attended the condo's annual meeting: "I thank you for financing my vacation in Greece. It was great. But your maintenance bills would be much lower if you just sat down and resolved your problems face-to-face rather than calling me first. Somehow, I'll find a way to pay for my vacation." Lawyers aren't always so candid, but litigation is always expensive. That's why a cooperative spirit is important to both the social and financial state of the association.

MAINTENANCE RESPONSIBILITIES: PROVIDING ESSENTIAL SERVICES

The most obvious of the board's responsibilities seems ridiculously easy to carry out: identifying the problem and then finding someone to fix it. Unfortunately, property management is seldom so simple. Here are some complications to consider when addressing these two "simple" matters.

Identifying the Problem

When a light goes out in the hall, the problem is obvious: A bulb needs replacing. But if there are brownish marks on the Smiths' ceiling, near the living room window, what's the problem? It could be a leaking radiator upstairs. It could be deteriorating mortar in the outside wall that lets the rain in. It could be a side effect of the broken pipe two floors up, since water sometimes travels inside the walls, along pipes and beams. It could just be a leak in the neighbor's waterbed or the poor quality of the Smiths' paint. So what's really the problem?

Your first line in sorting things out is a seasoned manager, an experienced custodian, or both. A knowledgeable professional who knows the building's eccentricities can usually diagnose problems correctly at a glance. In smaller condos, there is often a predilection for do-it-yourself in the name of saving money. But the salary of a part-time caretaker who lives nearby and can respond swiftly to emergencies is an investment in reliable, quick service and essential preventive maintenance. There are often legal and safety questions as well. If your building has a high-pressure steam boiler, for example, the fire laws may require you to hire a licensed operator to run it.

Another important technique for tracking problems back to their roots is a *service request book*. Not unlike a receipt book in format, it contains slips that can be torn out and deposited in a "request box" as well as carbonless or carbon-paper copies that remain permanently bound in the book. (If custom-printed books aren't readily available, a phone message book, of the type sold by any commercial stationer, will serve handily.) The board should check these records from time to time, both to ensure that repairs are being taken care of promptly and to look for patterns of failure that may point to a more serious problem or suggest a potentially money-saving preventive. For example, damaged window frames in a number of upper-floor apartments may point to leaks in the parapets surrounding the roof. Persistent electrical problems in a group of adjacent units may reflect a serious deficiency in the wiring. For the same reason, it's important to keep records of all work done; like mighty oaks, major headaches grow from modest beginnings.

Managing Service and Maintenance Employees

Whether you have only a part-time custodian or a sizable staff of handymen, porters, and doormen, it's important that each employee's responsibilities be clearly defined. Each worker should have a job description *in writing* (and in the employee's language, if that isn't English). The description should incorporate a schedule of routine tasks, like sweeping public areas, cutting the grass, and disposing of the garbage so that responsibility for these jobs is specifically assigned. Careful scheduling can also enhance the efficiency of overall operations. The board in one recently converted apartment house was planning to enlarge the staff, since the hallways never seemed to be adequately cleaned. After working out a detailed new cleaning schedule, though, they discovered that perfectly satisfactory results could be obtained simply by changing the schedules of the porters already on the payroll.

A careful examination of your needs may also point to possible staff reductions. Do you really need twenty-four-hour doorman coverage, or would just the evening hours suffice? Modernizing the trash compactors can free one porter to do the tasks you once needed two porters to handle. Installing a new control system for the boiler may enable the custodian to take on tasks you previously hired a part-time engineer to handle.

When planning employee work schedules, keep the owners' habits in mind. In this era of two-earner families, there is likely to be much greater demand on building services over the weekend, when everyone is home, than during the week, when nearly all residents are at work. To deal with this asymmetry, you may want to offer an extra day off to a porter willing to work weekends, or hire part-time help to handle Saturday and Sunday cleaning.

If your employees belong to a union, you'll find the conditions of their employment spelled out in great detail in your contract. A master contract is usually drawn up in negotiations with a large association of owners' groups and presented to other boards more or less as a fait accompli. If your board was not part of the negotiating unit, however, it should not feel obliged to accept an unsatisfactory package. While the union is unlikely to rewrite the entire master contract, it may consider modifying individual clauses to fit your particular situation. For example, if your management company offers a good health insurance plan, the union may be willing to let you substitute that one for its own. Or you could get permission to replace two part-time porters with one full-time porter. The flexibility of unions varies enormously: Some are consistently militant, some are always accommodating, others adapt their stands to shifting economic conditions. Managers and other boards who have dealt with your union can give you some indication of whether negotiations might bear fruit. When in doubt, start out with your dream plan, even if you know it will be unacceptable; the union is likely to take an equally extreme stand, and you will both have plenty of the "wiggle room" needed to reach a compromise.

At any point in relations with a union, it's important to keep good records. If you have a "problem" employee you would like to reform or discharge, send that person detailed reprimands in writing, and send copies to the union. After three or four months, you should either see an improvement in the worker's performance or dismiss him, using the reprimands as evidence of failure to perform.

Even if your staff is nonunion, there should be a clear understanding about hours, days off, vacations, annual pay reviews, insurance, and fringe benefits. Once the policy is set, however, a degree of flexibility is needed to make it work. A janitor who does repairs evenings and weekends—since that's when people are at home—shouldn't be begrudged a couple of hours off during the day. Of course, if your good nature is abused, it's back to the letter of the law.

If any current practices seem unreasonable (too much compensatory time off for Sunday work, say, or too little insurance coverage), ask your managing agent (or, if you are self-managed, your lawyer, accountant, or board members at other buildings in your neighborhood) what the customs are in your area. If you decide to make changes, be sure to do so gradually to avoid raising false expectations or stirring unnecessary resentment.

Who Fixes What?

This is an area of frequent confusion in shared-ownership developments. The division of responsibility between the association and the individual owner is spelled out in "The Book"—the code of regulations governing each association—and owners should read theirs carefully. As a general rule, the association maintains "common systems" (plumbing, wiring, roads and drives, etc.), and each owner pays to fix everything *inside* the unit (appliances, painting and decoration, etc.) In an apartment or town house development, this division usually makes the individual responsible for everything "from the paint out," while the condo handles the rest. In other words, the unit owner pays for decoration, furniture, and appliances, while the association maintains plumbing and wiring, stairs and hallways, and other systems shared by all owners. More specifically, if the drip is caused by a valve set in the wall, as in a shower stall, then the condo fixes it. But if the leaky valve is outside the wall, as over the kitchen sink, the individual owner fixes it. Many variations are possible, though, so be sure to check your own regulations for the definitive answer.

As a practical matter, residents usually turn first to the maintenance staff for minor repairs, and most associations extend this service as an accommodation to owners, charging only for parts used. Just what is a "minor repair"? Replacing a broken washer obviously qualifies, while retiling the entire kitchen floor does not. But what about replacing a broken faucet? Or fixing a leaky dishwasher? Try to anticipate these gray areas and build them into your guidelines, and provide a mechanism for dealing with cases that aren't clearly covered.

Even where owners know they are responsible for the work, they may ask the custodian to take it on as a "private" job. To prevent such work from interfering with essential maintenance tasks, there must be a clear definition of the custodian's duties and hours. If you have a larger staff, you might consider allowing employees to do any work residents request, subject to billing through the association. This policy has the virtue of simplicity, but it does increase administrative paperwork and overhead costs. And residents may, in fact, prefer the freedom to negotiate with contractors of their choice.

Major Repairs and Improvements

Some projects require more than a few hours' work by the maintenance staff: replacing the lobby chandelier, patching the roof, replacing leaking steam pipes, draining and resealing the pool, etc. The obvious approach is to hire an outside contractor to do the work, but this can be expensive. If members of the staff are willing to do the work—and can do it without shortchanging their other duties—it pays to give their offer some serious thought. Look at similar jobs they have done. If pipes are involved, has their other plumbing work been satisfactory? If painting or plastering is required, how good is their "finish" work? If it's satisfactory, and the bid is reasonable, take them up on it.

You'll enhance their commitment to the condo and save money, too.

If you choose to solicit bids from outside contractors, insist on three or more proposals. If the job is simple (e.g., replacing a trash compactor, repainting the halls), you can usually choose, on the basis of price alone, among bids which specify the same products. Be cautious with exceptionally low bids—those 15 to 20 percent less than the average. The contractor may have misunderstood the terms of bidding or may be excluding some of the preparatory work (e.g., wiring for compactors) or finishing work (e.g., plastering and painting a wall opened for plumbing work).

Ensuring that bids are, in fact, comparable becomes more difficult when the project is a complex one, like rebuilding elevators, reconstructing a leaky facade, or updating a boiler. That's when it's advisable to hire a consulting engineer or another outside specialist to draw up a "request for proposals," giving specific terms of the bid. The consultant should also assist in evaluating bids and drawing up a contract, inspect the work in progress, and give final approval to both progress and final payments. Chapter 5 has information on the financial aspects of negotiating a contract; the basic rule is to make sure you get what you pay for.

If you cannot afford or cannot find a reliable outside consulting engineer, or if you simply want more detailed information for your own analysis of the project, you can turn to your managing agent, invite exploratory bids, or both. Some large management firms have engineers on staff who can evaluate the situation; in other cases, the site manager's own experience can guide your decisions. "Exploratory bidding" is a technique for tapping the expertise of contractors in the field. You simply invite a number of firms to come in, inspect the problem, and recommend a solution in detailed proposals. Make it clear to the executive who comes to inspect the building that you want a step-by-step explanation of the work recommended and the materials to be used. The proposals are likely to differ widely when they come in. You will have to study them closely and phone or write the contractors for explanations of the differences. Don't hesitate to play one off against another. Tell Delilah

Contractors, "Samson Roofing says we just need patching; why do you recommend a complete replacement?" If Neptune Plumbing says the problem is a valve and Apollo says it's a pump, ask each bidder to explain how the conclusion was reached, then look at the situation yourself and see which one is more logical. Once you are satisfied that you understand what is needed and what can be omitted (your managing agent and owners of similar buildings can help a lot here), you should draw up a request for proposals of your own and seek a new round of bids, all of which conform to the specifications you establish.

How can you find contractors to bid on a specific project? If you have a consulting engineer or professional manager, that person should be able to supply a list of reliable companies. If most of the buildings in your neighborhood are of the same vintage, you can ask your neighbors how they dealt with similar problems. Keep your eyes open, as well. If you see work being done elsewhere in your neighborhood, look for the names of contractors on trucks, signs, or other equipment. If a job seems to be going well, stop and talk to the foreman or supervisor, get details about the company's background, and inspect the work more closely. Talk to the building's owner, too, for a firsthand report on the work. Don't hesitate to discuss your plans with friends who've had similar work done. The more information you get, the more comfortable you will feel with the final decision, and the more likely you are to be pleased with the results.

In some cases, a managing agent or a custodian may pressure the board to use a particular contractor, even without competitive bids. Such insistence should, to be blunt, arouse your suspicions. While it is possible that your manager has had exceptionally positive experiences with a particular contractor, it is also possible that this contractor buys favor with gratuities. Insist on at least three *written* bids for *every* contract, and consider outside consultation on the large ones. If your manager declines to provide this service, solicit the bids directly and start looking for a new manager. (See Chapter 4 for more information on the games managers play.)

LEGAL AND FINANCIAL RESPONSIBILITIES

Though this portion of the board's work is often invisible to other owners, it carries the potential of enormous risks. An error could jeopardize the stability of the entire association—and the value of its members' investments. At the same time, board members can be held personally responsible for their actions. They are *fiduciaries*, technically speaking, and could find themselves the target of lawsuits if one or more unit owners feel their interests have been harmed by board action. Here are some rules for ensuring that board actions are proper and prudent.

Find Professional Help

No association can successfully tend to its affairs without good legal and financial advice. And *good* in this case means "knowledgeable and experienced in the field." An attorney with a record of achievement in criminal law, no matter how illustrious, or an accountant specializing in municipal bonds, no matter how much money she's made for her clients, is not for you. Look for professionals with clients whose needs parallel your own. If yours is a first-class resort condo, look for experts who deal with other luxury developments. If you live in a modest middle-income urban condo, ask boards of nearby condos for recommendations. You'll often find the type of professionals you're looking for at local conferences or workshops on condo and co-op issues. Also look for notices in the mail or in the real estate section of your local newspapers. One board found an accountant who had, in fact, served as treasurer of a similar condo; the same board engaged an attorney referred by a local community action group. Even if a board member is a CPA or an LL.D., it's worth retaining independent counsel. An outside advisor can afford to offer objective, considered opinions without any taint of self-interest.

What should these people do for you? Your lawyer should be able to advise you in any situation: determining what records are required by law, evaluating contracts with managers or contractors, advising on legal (and illegal) uses of units, clarifying issues in disputes among owners. A lawyer who is knowledgeable in your state's real estate law and readily accessible by phone is much more useful than the corporate tax specialist in unit eighteen or a much-publicized courtroom star. In fact, a good lawyer is one who keeps you *out* of court, except as a last resort.

Similarly, an accountant should be willing to answer questions from board members and other shareholders and to explain reports in nontechnical terms. An accountant's primary responsibility is to prepare an audited financial statement each year and to alert the board to any irregularities. In addition, the accountant should keep you out of trouble with the authorities by preparing any tax returns or other financial reports not filed by the managing agent. A good financial counselor should also help you to make plans, advising on the impact of various money-raising strategies. Should you borrow money? Raise maintenance fees? Postpone work? Individual shareholders and the condo as a whole will benefit when this professional's knowledge and insight help guide the decision. (See Chapter 5, "Money Matters," for more details.)

There are a few pointers to keep in mind: You are dealing with busy professionals, so take care to avoid wasting their time and, in the process, your money. Think through your queries carefully so that you can pose precise questions and get useful, to-the-point answers. Be sure you have the key facts in hand, or can define the information you still need. When phoning, write out your questions in advance and keep the note pad in front of you when you call. When writing a letter, keep it short and succinct.

Keep Good Minutes

For present shareholders, for future board members, and for your lawyer, in case of any sort of dispute, it is essential that good minutes be kept at every board meeting. Keeping a permanent record of conversations among friends and neighbors seems odd at first, but there is no other way to create a record of decisions taken and the thinking behind them. This task normally falls to the secretary, but if you prefer, you can elect a "recorder" at the beginning of each meeting. In some cases, the managing agent may be willing to keep the record. The "who" is less important than the "what": a concise account of all the board's actions. (See page 173 for more ideas.)

What makes good minutes? Several styles are possible, ranging from a lively narrative that summarizes the meeting in an almost novelistic fashion to a spare outline that simply lists the topics discussed, identifies those who spoke "for" and "against," and records the results of any vote. One secretary used his computer to highlight formal actions and obligations for the next meeting. Style is the personal choice of the minute-taker, but one thing is essential: Whenever the board chooses to make a decision—to hire a contractor, to raise the common charges, to paint the halls, to approve alterations—whoever is taking minutes should insist that a member phrase the proposal as a formal motion. This motion (verbatim), the names of the persons who made it and seconded it, and the vote on it should all be carefully noted in the minutes. Not only does this step ensure accurate and complete minutes, it also ensures that all board members know precisely what they are voting for.

What becomes of the minutes? They should be distributed to all board members, preferably within a week of the meeting. A complete copy should also be kept in a loose-leaf binder for reference on demand. Any number of people may ask to see them: shareholders, prospective buyers, past and future board members, and lawyers for all interested parties. When it comes to minutes, the Boy Scouts have the right idea: Be prepared.

Regulating Owner Rentals and Sublets

Ideally, a shared-ownership development should be a community of owners, working together to solve common problems and meet common needs. The rapid turnover and short-term residence usually associated with rental tenants tend to undermine this ideal, and the governing documents of both condos and co-ops usually impose some restrictions on the practice. In some cases, specific rules and limits are spelled out; in other cases, the details are left to the board's discretion. Within these limits, however, it is important to establish a clearly articulated policy and make all owners aware of it.

In defining a policy, the board needs to balance the needs of both the association and the individual owners. In a very large development, for example, rentals are less disruptive. The budget usually covers full-time professional management, and the number of active owners—even if relatively small by proportion—can still be substantial. In fact, many units in such developments may be owned by investors who specifically intend to rent them out. In such circumstances, the board's principal concern is seeing that the lease conforms to condo policies and binds the tenant to the house rules.

Smaller developments present a different situation. When too many units are occupied by renters, a sense of shared interest and community can be impossible to achieve. In the worst case, board members find themselves serving as unpaid managing agents for their absent neighbors. In one twenty-eight-unit building where sublets had not been monitored, a newly elected board found that half the apartments were occupied by short-term renters. In an effort to regain some control, the board decided to impose a complete moratorium on new rentals. Careful planning and well-articulated policies can, however, help avoid such a dramatic step.

Among the regulations boards commonly establish (in so far as their regulations permit) are: a limit on the frequency with which a unit can be rented—no more than once in a two-year period, for example—a minimum and/or maximum term for a sublet, a cap on the number of units that can be sublet at any one time, board approval of lease terms, a sublet fee (see also page 110), and a board interview with the proposed tenant.

In deciding what requirements to impose, the board needs to consider the reasons owners might have to rent. In a resort area, for example, owners can rent out their units for a substantial profit during the high season. To keep the complex from taking on the character of a hotel, therefore, condo boards often set a three- or four-month minimum period for sublets, or limit each owner to one sublet a year, or both. There will still be "strangers" around during the season, but at least they will stay long enough to get involved in the community and owners will be encouraged to stay in residence for much of the year.

Boards in a large city confront different problems. An owner being temporarily reassigned by her employer may want to rent her unit for the two years she will be abroad. In a soft real estate market, a young couple who has moved to larger quarters may want to rent their old unit to cover the cost of carrying two mortgages until the unit is sold. In these circumstances, a board may want to impose a maximum term on sublets, to make sure a temporary situation doesn't become permanent. In the case of the couple who has moved out, the board may also insist that an option to purchase be part of any lease, to encourage both the old owners and the new tenants to think in terms of moving from rental to purchase as quickly as possible.

Should the board interview the prospective tenant? In a small building, this is virtually essential, since good relations among residents are among the board's most important responsibilities. In a large complex with a number of rentals, interviews can be a burden on the board, though they still provide a good opportunity to acquaint newcomers with the association.

Monitoring Resales

To assure that the wider interests of the association are protected whenever a unit changes hands, boards are almost always given some authority to examine and approve all proposed sales. Co-op boards and some condo boards (particularly in Florida) have the right to examine buyers' financial affairs, interview them, and accept or reject an application for almost any reason. Other condo boards have less sweeping powers, such as the right to review the contract of sale and to exercise a *right of first refusal* (i.e., to purchase the empty unit themselves by matching the buyer's offer) if they feel the sale would not be in the association's best interests. Sometimes the decision to exercise this right must be ratified, in each case, by a majority vote of the unit owners.

Regardless of how the board exercises its powers, there are some matters that should always be examined. Is there anything in the contract of sale that contradicts the association's regulations and by-laws? Does the new condo deed, for instance, include the restrictions required by the association charter? (See page 136.) Is it clear the buyer plans to live in the unit and not rent it out (unless, of course, the association allows investors to buy in)? Has the buyer read the house rules and formally agreed to accept them? Are the price and financial terms reasonable for current market conditions? If the price is exceptionally low, the sale may tend to pull down the value of other owners' units. If the terms are unusually generous—no down payment, a large second mortgage—the buyer's ability to meet future financial obligations may be open to question. The board should be satisfied with the answers to all of these questions before agreeing to permit the sale.

One problem area in which the board's powers are limited is learning about sales in advance. Fearing delay, sellers, buyers, and sometimes even brokers try to avoid attracting the board's attention and may not contact the association until the sale is a fait accompli. There are several ways to prevent this from happening. First of all, the board should make an effort to handle all requests for information or approval as expeditiously as possible. A board member might also contact local real estate brokers to make them aware of this commitment to efficiency. Be sure to stress the board's willingness to answer questions and provide information to prospective buyers; this strategy not only encourages professionals to cooperate with you but also ensures that new owners are better informed. You may even want to offer to organize interviews on an informal basis to enable buyers to have their questions answered and, in the process, to enable the board to get to know new residents. (See page 79 for suggestions on conducting interviews.) In addition, there are other ways to keep track of sales: reading real estate ads regularly, asking the building staff to notify the board of visits by real estate salespeople, and above all, maintaining good neighborly relations that encourage owners to discuss their plans with board members.

Where a screening interview is required, there's no trouble about being notified—the sale can't be closed without the board's written approval—but often there are questions about how this power is used. It's probably the best-publicized and least-understood part of a board's job. The gossip columns all reported, for example, that the rock star Madonna was turned down by a Manhattan co-op. Few accounts explained, however, that the board in question acted not out of dislike for the singer but out of a desire to keep crowds of paparazzi out of the lobby. Similarly, an elegant Park Avenue co-op rejected former President Richard Nixon—a man most of the residents greatly admired—when the board learned that security measures proposed by the Secret Service would affect every aspect of the residents' lives, from when they could throw a party to when they could use the elevator. Whether the applicant is famous or obscure, a board's primary concern is protecting the investments and the comfort of the association's members. In practice, most buyers consider the full range of obligations they are assuming, make an effective presentation, and receive quick approval.

When the regulations give the board the power to screen applicants, it can usually act "for any reason or for no reason," and the grounds for each decision are not normally disclosed. But to keep internal discussions logical, fair, and consistent, the board should base its decision on objectively defined criteria, like inconvenience to other unit owners, inadequate financial resources, or a plan to rent the unit contrary to association policy. Keep in mind, too, that civil rights laws at the federal, state, and local level forbid using race, religion, national origin, age, or marital status as the *sole* grounds of rejection; some localities add sex, sexual preference, and profession to the list of impermissible criteria. If a rejected applicant files a formal complaint with the local office of the Civil Rights Commission, it's helpful to be able to cite sound reasons clearly related to the welfare of the association. Your lawyer can provide details on the specific rules and procedures in your area.

All these rules sound quite logical in the abstract, but

when you start applying them to real life, motives tend to overlap. It may be illegal, for example, to refuse an applicant solely on the grounds that he is an accountant, but it is perfectly permissible to do so if he intends to practice in his apartment, bringing a high level of traffic into the building. A woman cannot be denied the right to purchase simply because she is a single mother, but if her income is not adequate to cover mortgage, maintenance, and day-care expenses, her application may properly be questioned on financial grounds. Weigh these matters carefully; since rejections are relatively rare, one or two actions can take on a great deal of importance. If a board refuses only two applicants in the course of a year, but both of them are black gay men, the board may find itself the object of unwanted attention from the agencies charged with enforcing civil rights laws, to say nothing of protest groups.

An emotional, rather than rational, response can sometimes harm the entire association. One co-op board decided to "punish" an uncooperative shareholder who constantly paid late, refused to participate in buildingwide projects, and made unauthorized alterations by refusing to approve a buyer when she chose to sell. This reaction may make the board feel better, but the results are counterproductive: Blocking the sale embitters relations and prolongs the struggle; approving the sale gets the disruptive force out of the association. Furthermore, such an action violates the board's fiduciary responsibilities to the shareholder and could easily become grounds for a lawsuit. Finally, if a board gets a reputation for being arbitrary and difficult, local real estate brokers may become reluctant to show units for sale in the development.

For the screening process to work well, it is necessary to gather information that will determine whether or not the prospective buyer would be a solid member of your community. Look critically at the application form you are using. Does it address the questions you need answered? Does it yield the kind of information you need? Could some information be more easily obtained elsewhere? For example, if you request a copy of the mortgage application, you can skip a lot of financial information on your own form. Today, most purchasers buy in with a mortgage, and the

application shows not only what figures the bank is working with but also how tight the applicants' finances really
are. On your own form there are three "musts": social security numbers for both buyers and sellers (since you must
report the transaction to the IRS), future address of the
seller (for his or her copy of that report), and a copy of
the contract of sale, so that you can track both the type of
improvements included by the seller or demanded by the
buyer and the current sale prices. Also, asking for the contract ensures that you interview only serious buyers who
have, in fact, taken the transaction that far.

Confirm the basic data furnished by the applicant by
speaking with employers, prior landlords or neighbors, and
other references. In many parts of the country, commercial
services can do this research for you. The fee (typically $50
or $75) is passed along directly to the applicant. If you have
a managing agent, that company may be willing to perform
the checks for you on the same terms as an outside contractor.

Interviews with prospective buyers give you a chance to
clarify any ambiguities on the application form and to become acquainted with the applicants on a personal level. To
set an appropriately relaxed tone, start with fairly innocent
questions like, "Why did you choose this neighborhood?" or
"What attracted you to this building?" Once the interview is
under way, don't be afraid to raise delicate questions. If there
is a curious gap between college and employment, ask why.
If the applicants' indebtedness seems high, ask how they plan
to deal with it. There will never be a better occasion for raising these issues, and a decision is much easier if you are satisfied you have all the information in hand.

In addition to seeking information, board members can
use the interview as a forum for introducing a new association member to its goals and plans. Questions like "What
role would you like to play in the association?" or "Given
your knowledge of accounting, would you be willing to serve
on our audit committee?" are appropriate at this time. If
new shareholders come into the complex expecting to play
a role in its operations, they are likely to be much more
involved once they move in.

In the course of the screening process, an applicant

may press you to short-cut your deliberations and come to an instant decision. In responding, stress the fact that board members are fiducaries acting on behalf of *all* owners. Once you have established certain procedures to fulfill this duty, you must adhere to them in fairness to all the other purchasers who have met the criteria. Usually, this argument will persuade the applicants to be patient. If they continue to press, the best response is: "If you want an *immediate* response, the answer is 'No.' If you want a *careful and considered* response, you'll have to wait until we complete our checks and the interview."

LEARNING FROM OTHERS

Comparing notes and trading tips with other members of shared-ownership housing associations can often help everyone find solutions for common problems. Here are some of the ways board members and other owners interested in association activities can meet their counterparts locally.

On the grass roots level, a few inquiries among unit owners in nearby complexes can yield the names of board members and officers in your neighborhood; an informal get-together could be organized in someone's yard or garden during the summer. You're also likely to meet neighbors who share your interests at local churches, or at block- or civic-association meetings. In fact, if your community has a number of condo or co-op developments, the association may well have a special "condo committee' that can supply a convenient forum for exchanging information— the names of reliable contractors, for example, or techniques for controlling the Japanese beetles in everyone's garden—and for dealing jointly with local authorities on matters from garbage collection to tax assessments. If you're not sure what groups exist in your neighborhood, read the community weekly newspaper, look for posters in shopping malls, or ask a local realtor.

There are also more formal ways to find information and support. In some cities with a large number of shared-ownership developments, the suppliers of various essential services often organize workshops for board members and other leaders. A specialist law firm or a local bar association might organize one on "Current Issues in Condominium Law." A large pool maintenance contractor or a local trade association might invite you to a half-day session on "Swimming Pool Problems and Solutions." These workshops are usually quite professionally mounted, with expert commentators, helpful displays, and plenty of literature to take home. More often than not, they're free of any charge; the organizer expects to recoup the cost from the additional business these sessions generate. There's the rub, of course: The advice offered is knowledgeable but hardly disinterested. Go, listen, analyze the questions raised from the perspective of *your* association, but don't sign any contracts until you're satisfied it's a service you actually need, provided on terms satisfactory to you. You'll find announcements of these workshops in the real estate section of your local newspapers or among the many fliers and brochures mailed to the association.

Another way to learn more about shared-ownership housing is to attend a short-term course at a local university or community college. Phone and ask about continuing education or real estate institute courses. It's not uncommon to find a course especially designed for newly elected board members that runs over a weekend or three or four evenings. In addition, there are often courses on maintenance problems which board or committee members might want to attend. Retirees from the North, for example, might want to take a course on landscaping in Florida or Arizona. Some associations pay the fees involved, but such an expense can put a big dent in the budgets of small associations.

Courses and workshops are also organized by specialized condo and co-op associations. Most metropolitan areas have one or more local groups that offer newsletters, consulting services, and other opportunities to exchange information city- or statewide. They also represent the interests of shared-ownership housing in political and policy-making forums at city hall, the state capitol, and in Washington. Your lawyer, civic group, or members of other boards should be able to put you in touch with a local organization. You're also likely to learn about these groups by reading articles on co-op and condo issues in the real estate section of your local newspaper.

In addition, there are two organizations that provide similar services on a nationwide scale. Individual condo, co-op, and homeowners associations can join either or both directly, or through affiliated local groups. The Community Associations Institute (1423 Powhattan Street, Alexandria, VA 22314; phone 800-342-5224) is essentially a professional organization of property managers, both paid and volunteer; membership is comprised of board officers, real estate professionals, lawyers, accountants, and a variety of suppliers. CAI publishes newsletters and a wide range of books; it also organizes conferences on condo and co-op issues in various parts of the country. Costs can be relatively high, but the information offered is encyclopedic. Founded in 1973, CAI has served primarily large middle-class and luxury properties, though it is seeking to expand its services to smaller developments by offering more favorable terms and practical services.

The National Association of Housing Cooperatives (1614 King Street, Alexandria, VA 22314; phone 703-549-5201) began as a network of subsidized middle- and low-income co-ops; today, any co-op or condo may join. Its services—including relatively inexpensive nontechnical publications, national and regional conferences, staff consultations on specific issues, and referrals to local professionals—are particularly helpful to small, self-managed developments. The NAHC also serves as an active lobbyist for shared-ownership housing, appearing before congress and federal agencies to protect the broad interests of associations and unit owners. In recent years, for example, NAHC has challenged Internal Revenue Service rulings that increased the tax liabilities of many co-ops and condos.

Membership fees in both local and national groups are scaled to the size of the association: typically, a base amount of about $50 plus a "per unit" charge of, say, $2. As with the purchase of any other service, a board should weigh the potential benefits against the costs involved. A recently established condo, for example, may find the support especially useful; an older association with a pool of experienced leaders on its board and committees may prefer to allocate its resources elsewhere.

The most important decision concerning allocating resources, though, will be the one involving building management—the subject of the next chapter.

4
Day-to-Day Management:
Choosing the Right Approach

Running a residential complex on a day-to-day basis is a demanding job, and the management concerns are the same whether you live in a condo, co-op, or planned community. It's not that the individual problems themselves are difficult to solve but that they just keep on coming. As the old saying goes, "It's one damned thing after another," with little, if any, respite. Keeping abreast of routine tasks, tracking finances, responding to owner complaints, and attending to long-term maintenance is so difficult to do on a part-time basis that most associations turn to outside professional management. While this approach eases the headaches, it does involve costs, both tangible and intangible. Self-management is often an attractive option for small and medium-sized buildings, and hiring your own manager is often the best approach for large developments. Here are the pros and cons of each method.

OUTSIDE PROFESSIONAL MANAGEMENT

It's easy to see why so many associations choose this option: It affords access to professional support at lower cost than engaging such a staff directly and with fewer burdens than self-management. The managing agent you hire should send a site manager to the property regularly to oversee routine maintenance, have a representative in attendance at all regular board and membership meetings, and handle all routine financial and legal affairs. The cost will vary from city to city, but annual fees of $200 to $500 per unit (i.e., $10,000 to $25,000 for a fifty-unit complex) were common in 1988. From the owners' point of view, that's $16.67 to $41.67 of an average unit's monthly common charges.

So why shouldn't everyone just join the bandwagon? First of all, there's the money. The sums involved can put a dent in a tight budget, and in the case of small buildings, there may be a minimum fee that works out to a much larger sum on a per-unit basis. Then there are the hidden costs. The boom in shared-ownership housing has caused an explosive growth in the number of management companies—without a concommitant increase in the number of qualified managers. As a result, there is a real risk of getting stuck with an inadequate, incompetent, or even corrupt managing agent. The search for an efficient and reliable managing agent can be time-consuming, and the board and unit owners must devote considerable effort to monitoring the manager.

Here's a worst-case scenario, with some lessons to be drawn.

A new board, with a mandate to hire a new managing agent, was elected at 3550 Highland Road. The board members decided to begin their search with friends on the boards of other condos in the same neighborhood. On the basis of their recommendations, the board selected three companies to interview; all of them sent representatives to the building. The vice-president of Global Management did a quick tour of the facilities, accompanied by the chief custodian, and made a desultory presentation to the board. He was clearly well-versed in management but did not seem particularly eager to take a building in the Highland area. The president of Bluebird Management made no effort to get to know the building, but her presentation to the board was impressive: thorough, confident, knowledgeable. Spier-Hart Realty, a large, well-known firm, sent three executives: the director of operations, the head of the condominium division, and a senior site manager. They spent two hours inspecting the building the day before the interview and made a detailed and persuasive presentation.

When the formal proposals came in, the board found itself in a quandary. Bluebird made the lowest bid by far; Spier-Hart's was 50 percent higher; and Global was in the middle. The board sought to negotiate a lower fee with Spier-Hart, but the company was inflexible. Global hinted at compromise, but the board was not convinced the firm could meet its needs. The board therefore chose Bluebird, which had received an enthusiastic recommendation from another neighborhood board, despite some misgivings about its "low-ball" bid.

The problems began immediately. The site manager assigned by Bluebird antagonized the chief custodian with his imperious manner and monopolized board meetings with long-winded disquisitions on the mechanics of steam valves. Then he stopped coming to the building altogether. The first month's financial report never arrived. The Bluebird office moved to a new address without informing the condo; important mail, including bills and checks, was lost or delayed. The Bluebird president came to a board meeting, introduced a new site manager, and promised that the new office facilities would permit more efficient operations. The new manager proved much more helpful than her predecessor, but financial data were still slow to appear. No two oil deliveries came from the same company. Finally, the newspaper reported that Bluebird's principal stockholder was about to declare bankruptcy. The manager phoned to say she had given her notice to Bluebird. And the board found itself managing the building on its own.

The Right and Wrong Way to Search for a Managing Agent

How did the Highland board get into such a mess? First of all, they restricted their search to too few companies. The tactic of seeking recommendations was a good one, but personal contacts are merely one of the potential sources. Lawyers, accountants, the local association of co-ops and condos, even your chief custodian, drawing on his connections in the local grapevine, may provide you with advice on which companies to contact and which ones to avoid. It's not necessary to interview every candidate, but a preliminary investigation can help you identify leads worth pursuing.

Ask for written proposals so you can get a sense of each company's strengths and weaknesses. Does the company specialize in shared-ownership developments? Does it work only for board-run developments, or does it also manage rental properties and sponsor conversions? How many properties does each site manager have to handle? How many associations does each bookkeeper serve? Does the company have other clients in your neighborhood, or would you be an out-of-the-way stop? If these questions aren't answered in the literature, ask them at the interview.

Compare responses from company to company, too. If Company X assigns only four sites to a manager while Company Y assigns six, you can expect the bid from X to be higher. But you may be willing to pay the higher fee for the additional service. A management company in California takes an unusual approach: It bills clients by the hour for site managers' time. Boards can decide how much responsibility they will accept themselves and how much they are willing to pay a manager to assume responsibility for them. To get a sense of the "fit" of personalities and management philosophies, ask to meet the manager who would be assigned to your building. While the company may be unwilling to guarantee that a specific employee will be assigned to your development, they should be able to introduce at least one manager routinely assigned to properties like yours. The weight you assign each factor will depend on your individual situation, but take the time to consider all aspects of the decision. As so often in life, you get pretty much what you pay for.

Background checks are certainly in order. Ask for and verify business references. Try to visit one or two properties that the company manages, talking to both board members and a few ordinary residents. Ask about professional organizations. A company that belongs to the local board of realtors and groups like the Accredited Management Organization has shown a desire to maintain the respect of its peers. And while this is not, in itself, a guarantee of satisfaction, it does reflect a familiarity with and commitment to sound business practices.

Finally, take a close look at the draft contract and get your lawyer's reading, too. Make sure it covers all the services described below, under "What a Good Managing Agent Should Do." If an agent agrees to provide a special service (such as attending extra meetings during the first month), be sure it's guaranteed in writing. And insist on a cancellation clause that allows you to terminate the agreement for any reason on no more than sixty—preferably thirty—days' notice. Don't sign a contract on the oral promise that "we'll fix that later." The contract should spell out everything essential to you *before* it's submitted for signing.

When negotiating the contract, you must be prepared to call the deal off if a prospective managing agent is unwilling to address what you consider legitimate concerns. On some points, like the number of weekly visits from the site manager, compromise may be necessary. But the agent should make some gesture—like offering extra site visits during the first few months—to show a sincere desire to satisfy you. This late in the selection process, the thought of having to start over again is difficult and psychologically painful. Nevertheless, a willingness to take such a step is essential to maintaining your bargaining leverage.

How to Spot Trouble with a Manager

The Highland board had several warnings that could have saved it trouble later on. When problems with the site manager arose, the board should have demanded a replacement without delay. As a practical matter, building management is only as good as the person in charge of day-to-day operations. Even if Highland's problems were matters more of personal style than professional substance, a change was in order. Close collaboration among manager, board, and building staff is essential, and distrust or animosity can slow or stall work as surely as a utility failure.

A warning sign of even more serious trouble was the failure to furnish financial reports and bank statements on schedule. The rapid turnover in oil suppliers was another tip-off to possible financial mismanagement. Money that should have gone to pay bills promptly may have been diverted to other purposes. What action should a board take when the figures are awry or missing? To start out, the board should protest to the site manager and follow up with phone calls and letters directly to the head of the management company. Next, a pointed letter from the condo's lawyer should remind the agent of the company's responsibility. If there's no adequate response, an unannounced visit to the agent's offices to inspect your records— the property of the condo, not the agent—should provide either definitive reassurance or proof that your concern is well founded.

And while patience is a virtue, inaction can be costly, in time and trouble as well as in cash. The longer an irregularity persists, the harder it will be to straighten out the books. If errors are not corrected within thirty days, invoke the cancellation clause in your contract and start looking for a new manager right away. It doesn't matter how pleasant, concerned, and articulate the front-office people are if your money is being mishandled and your property mismanaged.

What a Good Managing Agent Should Do

An agent should provide all these services, which should be spelled out in the contract:

1. *Regular supervision by a site manager.* The manager should visit the property several times a week to check on routine work, order necessary supplies, ensure that em-

ployees are carrying out association policies, advise the board on any needed work or projects, assist in soliciting and evaluating bids, and handle complaints from unit owners.

2. *Regular financial accounting.* This includes a monthly summary of income and expenditures, a detailed list of all checks issued, copies of all paid bills, a copy of the reconciled bank statement of your account, and reports on bills payable and owners in arrears. Needless to say, this accounting should show that your obligations are being met routinely and on time!

3. *All record-keeping and paperwork necessary to satisfy legal requirements.* The agent should ensure that all necessary permits, licenses, and certificates are kept up to date. In collaboration with your accountant, the agent's bookkeeper should also prepare and distribute an annual financial report and an accounting of tax-deductible expenses included in the common charges. Other financial services should include maintaining proper payroll accounts, paying taxes, and completing withholding forms for all association employees.

4. *Advice on major projects, tax policies, and employee relations.* An agent's professional expertise should be available to help you plan and execute capital improvements, take advantage of any local tax savings programs, and maximize the productivity of your employees. While an additional fee may be charged for special services, like an extensive engineering study, counsel on the day-to-day operations of the property should be included in the basic fee.

5. *Services related to the purchase and sale of units.* Representing the association at closings, acting as broker for owners who wish to sell, and, in the case of co-ops, making necessary background checks are services that may be provided by the managing agent. Custom varies from city to city; in many parts of the country, only independent real estate agents or attorneys provide theses services. When offered, they generally involve an extra fee or commission, paid by one of the individuals involved, not the association. The seller, for example, usually pays the broker's commission and closing fee; the applicant pays the research fee for background checks.

The Sponsor as Managing Agent

If your development was constructed in the last few years or only recently converted to shared ownership, the developer or sponsor of the conversion may still be acting as managing agent. Especially in large complexes, it is not uncommon for the sponsor/developer to remain in charge indefinitely. This state of affairs may be good or bad, and a board needs to examine the question coolly and rationally. The board should not automatically fire the sponsor simply because some negotiations about the conversion were difficult, because there were delays in the construction work, or because the condo next door did it. Similarly, a board should not retain an unsatisfactory manager simply because the firm "knows the property." The key question is whether service meets residents' expectations. Before undertaking a transition from sponsor to outside management, however, the following issues must be considered:

1. *Is an organized and active board in place?* The transition to a new managing agent makes considerable demands on board members: identifying and screening potential managers, negotiating contracts, working with new personnel, and establishing clear-cut policies. The association must be "mature" enough to have able people on the board and to have a clear consensus for change.

2. *What is the sponsor's role on the board?* From Boston to Berkeley, many cities and states protect rental tenants from eviction when a complex is converted to shared ownership. In such cases, the sponsor usually retains ownership of these apartments and therefore controls several board seats. A sponsor who holds a majority of the seats, of course, can choose the managing agent, no matter what the residents want. A sponsor in a minority position, however, may vote only in proportion to the number of shares held. Hiring an outside agent may lead to awkward negotiations, but they can be brought to a satisfactory conclusion if both residents and sponsor concentrate on their shared interest in maintaining a high level of services for all residents.

3. *Is the developer/sponsor principally an investor or an operator?* If the company's prime motivation is the profit to

be made from development or conversion, it may allocate only limited resources to management and provide you with little in the way of day-to-day support. In such cases, the sponsor may actually welcome being replaced by an active board and outside managing agent who will relieve him of the headaches involved in running your building. On the other hand, some sponsors see their new properties as continuing sources of long-term management revenues. Such "developer-managers" often provide excellent service and need not be replaced unless efforts to improve service fail and the board is convinced it has found a management company that can do the job better.

4. *Is the sponsor/manager financially responsible?* In the vast majority of cases, the answer is "Yes," but it takes only one irresponsible developer to cost association members dearly in a property where a large number of unsold units remain in the developer's hands. If the developer holds 60 percent of the units, for example, he pays 60 percent of the common charges. The loss of this much revenue could force the association to double common charges paid by the other unit owners simply to cover basic expenses. In the case of a co-op with a large underlying mortgage, such a shortfall could lead to default—and the loss of all owners' equity. This is precisely what happened in the Northeast in 1990, when a decline in real estate values pushed some highly leveraged developers into bankruptcy.

The trouble signs are the same as those with any agent: a failure to furnish regular financial statements, statements submitted without backup documentation like paid bills and canceled checks, frequent and inexplicable changes in suppliers, delays in making routine payments like utilities, staff payroll, or the mortgage. If the board has any cause for concern, it should consider making an unannounced visit to the developer/manager's office, asking to see the property's financial records. These records are legally the property of the association and, under standard business practice, must be available to the association's officers any time during normal business hours. If you are not satisfied with what you see, come back with an accountant or a lawyer to help you. Certainly, you should retain legal counsel if you find evidence of a failure of the developer/manager to fulfill his obligations. Quick action can often minimize the potential loss, and the sooner you start negotiating with creditors the more flexible they are likely to be.

SELF-MANAGEMENT

Self-management offers the obvious advantage of the greatest possible control at a potentially lower expense. But financial costs are not the only consideration. Particularly during the transition phase, services may be less responsive than they had been previously under outside management. In addition, unit owners may have to devote more time and effort to running the property. The board should explore all the implications of the step and discuss them with the owners at a general meeting *before* taking any formal action.

Apportioning Responsibilities

Small buildings that choose self-management usually decide to divide the work among board members or owners on a project-by-project basis: One board member takes responsibility for the heating system, another takes charge of plumbing repairs, a third takes on finances, etc. It may be necessary to switch tasks around on an experimental basis before finding the right balance. This system has the advantage of spreading the burden of management, but it does create some administrative problems. First of all, each board member must be equally committed, so that tasks can, in fact, be shared equitably. Furthermore, this commitment must extend over several years, so that time is not lost constantly "retraining" new members. In addition, the board must meet fairly often—preferably once a week—in order to make sure that projects are properly coordinated. If the plumbing job runs over budget, the treasurer needs to make plans for dealing with the extra expense. If other jobs also run over budget, the entire board may need to consider an increase in common charges or a special assessment (see Chapter 5, "Money Matters"), and the sooner such plans are made, the more flexibility the board will have.

Naming a Resident Manager

The alternative to sharing management among board members is to designate one particular resident as the building manager. This person—preferably *not* a board member in order to separate policy making from operations—then takes primary responsibility for all management tasks, reporting to the board much as an outside manager would. Finding such a person is obviously a difficult task. Who has the willingness and the temperament to do the job, the freedom to make a multiyear commitment, and enough time available (preferably in the building) during business hours? A retired person, a full-time homemaker, or someone who works at home would all be likely candidates. Some buildings turn to retired board members or a resident with experience in real estate. This sort of background is useful, but it is not essential. Tenant-sponsored co-ops in some inner-city neighborhoods have flourished under the management of grandmothers with only high-school educations as well as energetic immigrants with only a limited knowledge of English. Anyone willing to make the commitment can usually learn the ropes in the course of a year.

Compensating a Manager

A more difficult decision concerns compensation. If your building is fairly large—say twenty-five or thirty units—managing is really a half-time job, and some sort of compensation may be not only a matter of fairness but also an absolute necessity to induce anyone to take the job. Some condos offer an outright fee; others waive common charges on the manager's apartment. In smaller buildings, a partial rebate of common charges or free utilities may suffice. Before reaching a decision, discuss all the possibilities—including the tax implications for the manager—with your lawyer and your accountant. If you are offering compensation, the manager cannot be a board member; doing so could jeopardize the association's special tax status.

Getting Specialized Help

Certain tasks, especially financial record-keeping, can be easily farmed out to a specialized service. Sending out bills and collecting carrying charges, recording payments and tracking arrears—all are part of routine rent collection as offered by many large banks and payroll services. These same suppliers can also prepare your payroll checks and records and can ensure that taxes are paid. Start by discussing your needs with the bank that holds one or more of your accounts, then approach competitive banks and services like Automatic Data Processing. Ask other self-managed developments about their experiences and recommendations. There is usually a setup fee, which includes training for your treasurer and manager, in addition to monthly charges for routine services. Solicit competitive bids, as for any major contract, and weigh each proposal carefully.

There are some additional factors to consider, too. If your manager or treasurer is willing to take on the work, you might consider buying a small computer for the condo. Add a simple bookkeeping program, a word-processing program, and a high-quality printer, and for as little as $3,000 (1988 prices), you can have all the equipment needed to prepare official notices, track expenses, and prepare financial reports. This one-time expense is probably less than one or two years' fees to an accounting service, but, of course, you are supplying the time and effort to make it work.

Figuring the Costs

To make sure self-management is really the best choice for you, calculate the total cost of your self-management package—manager's compensation, fees for outside services, office supplies and equipment purchased—and compare it to the cost of hiring outside management. There may or may not be financial savings; your final decision may turn on the value you assign the increased control and attention gained.

HIRING YOUR OWN MANAGER

In large developments—generally two hundred units or more—this approach can offer the control of self-management and the professionalism of an outside firm. It also offers some of the headaches of both, particularly those of identifying a good candidate and managing administrative expenses. If you are considering the transition from outside to inside management, it's best to deal with practical and financial considerations first.

Establishing a Budget

Take all of the services you need and calculate their costs one by one. To estimate figures, look at your current expenses, discuss typical costs with board members at similar developments in your area, and ask your local co-op or condo association for advice.

1. *Site Manager.* Your key person, responsible for day-to-day operations. The salary you offer should be high enough to appeal to an experienced manager; local real estate agents as well as board members in similar developments should be able to give you an idea of an appropriate figure. In addition, you'll have to factor in taxes (social security, unemployment, workers' compensation) and fringe benefits (health insurance, vacation, holiday bonus)—costs which normally add 25 to 30 percent to salary expenses. You also need to decide whether a one-person office will suffice, or whether your manager will require clerical or secretarial help. A support staff to handle details can free your manager to deal personally with problems, although even part-time secretarial salaries can add up to a substantial sum.

2. *Financial Services.* You can hire an outside accountant to handle all your financial tasks, you can keep them all in-house by adding a full-time or part-time bookkeeper

to your payroll, or you can take a hybrid approach, "farming out" the tasks of collecting carrying charges and preparing payrolls while asking the board treasurer to pay regular bills and keep financial records. The latter approach is likely to be the least costly in terms of cash, but it does require an active treasurer who is willing to work closely with the manager and ensure that the bank or payroll service lives up to its obligations. Hiring an accountant to do all the work reduces the burden on the board—and may be the best course if no board member feels comfortable in dealing with numbers—but it can create substantial ongoing expenses.

3. *Office Equipment and Supplies.* Self-management means paying your own overhead. You probably already have a furnished office on-site, but you may want to add some equipment to make your manager's life easier. For example, if you're considering in-house bookkeeping, you will probably want to factor in the cost of a small computer system to ease the task. Don't forget a good-quality printer to prepare bills, notices, newsletters, and correspondence. And when it comes to printing, you may want to replace the small "convenience" copier with a larger model capable of printing notices and newsletters. Check the rates at a local copy service first to see how soon your savings would earn back the investment.

This type of office equipment is usually depreciated over a period of five years, and you can use this standard for comparing a lump-sum capital investment to the cost of year-by-year services. In other words, the added cost of that larger copier shouldn't exceed five times what you'd spend running off notices at a local print shop. If you choose to finance the purchase over time, of course, you'll have a precise monthly figure to work with. Stationery, blank checks, copier supplies, and similar expenses are relatively minor, but they must be factored in for a realistic picture of your costs.

4. *"Hidden" Expenses.* Shifting from a management company to in-house management may deprive you of certain economies of scale—bulk oil purchasing, for example, or a special rate from a pool maintenance company that serves all the manager's developments. You are also likely

to seek advice more often from your lawyers and accountants, with a resulting increase in their fees. Be sure to include an allowance for these and other miscellaneous expenses in your budget estimates.

Once you have all these figures, you can compare them with the fee you are now paying a management company and get an idea of the financial consequences of hiring your own manager. The final decision, though, may hang on intangible factors: the advantages of having a manager responsible directly to the owners, the assurance that board policies will be promptly implemented, the enhanced control over every aspect of association affairs. The board will have to decide for itself what value to place on these advantages. Some developments have adopted a hybrid system, with an on-site manager, hired and paid directly by the board, who works in cooperation with an outside management firm that supplies all other services.

Finding a Manager

Whether you're converting to in-house management or simply seeking a replacement for your current manager, there are several sources you can tap to build a list of candidates. A good place to start is the people who know developments similar to yours. Board members at other condos may be able to offer recommendations, and your own staff may know of good managers in the neighborhood. Local real estate agents may have recommendations, too. The prospect of exchanging the migratory existence of a management company's staff for a stay-put job may attract a manager already working in your part of town. If you're converting from outside management, you may find a candidate in the site manager assigned to your complex by your present management company.

Be sure to interview several candidates, so you can get a feel for the talent available. You'll want someone experienced in managing your type of property: When there is no experienced boss to offer advice, on-the-job training just isn't possible. Familarity with building systems and local suppliers is important, too. But you should give particular emphasis to matters of personality. Can you see yourself working every day with this particular candidate? Would the prospect work well with your maintenance staff? With the owners? Skills and experience are only as good as the person delivering them.

No matter what type of management you choose, the process of carefully analyzing your needs is an important step in making sure you have found the best management approach for your complex.

5
Money Matters:
Making Ends Meet, Managing Your Assets

Handling money in a shared-ownership development can be the source of many problems that have only a handful of solutions. With few and limited exceptions, the association's resources consist of its owners, period. This fact poses particular dangers in associations where most unit owners are accustomed to renting, since it is not a landlord's deep pockets but the residents' own bank accounts which must be tapped whenever money is needed. And it is not the landlord but the board which must establish budgets and control expenditures. Here are the main points to keep in mind in managing the finances of shared-ownership complexes.

SOURCES OF FUNDS

Common Charges ("Maintenance")

This is the familiar sum, analogous to rent, due each month from all owners. When a development is first built or converted to joint ownership, the initial charge is set by the simple, straightforward process of dividing the total projected budget for the first year proportionally among the units. The result is divided into monthly installments as the first year's maintenance charge.

Once the development is up and running, changes in the charge are usually calculated on a proportional basis. For example, the Green Hill Condominium had run on a very closely balanced budget in 1986. On the basis of projections by its accountants and its managing agent, the board anticipated cost increases of 6 percent. The board therefore voted a 6 percent increase in common charges to make sure that income in 1987 would be sufficient to cover expenses.

There are, however, several alternative strategies that a board may wish to adopt. The most radical is the *zero-based system*. This approach is actually a re-creation of the conditions that existed when joint ownership began. The board establishes a specific budget for each category of expense based on past experience, the advice of a managing agent or board members in similar developments, and projections of reliable suppliers. After adding an allowance for unexpected contingencies, the total is divided proportionally among the owners. This approach is clearly the most rational, but it is also the most difficult and time-consuming.

The *scheduled-increase system* seeks to make increases more manageable by scheduling them at regular intervals. To avoid "price shocks," the development routinely increases common charges by a fixed percentage, say 4.5 percent (slightly higher than the last decade's average inflation rate), each year. The theory is that the surplus earned in years when actual costs rise more slowly than the increase in maintenance charges can be set aside to offset the deficit in years when costs rise faster than charges.

This system has an obvious danger: The relationship between income and expenses becomes muddied. The availability of excess funds may tempt the development to make desirable but unnecessary and expensive changes, like an elaborate landscaping project. With lots of money in the bank, it's hard to spot instances where it may be misspent. On the other hand, if unexpected costs arise—or if costs increase rapidly before a substantial reserve has been built up—the development will have trouble paying its bills. Before instituting planned increases, therefore, the board should have both an adequate reserve on hand (see below for more details) and clearly formulated plans for investing any surpluses. Owners should not hesitate to ask where these funds are held and what return they are earning.

At the same time, this system has a substantial advantage: Owners can better arrange their family budgets to cope with the modest planned increase, and the tensions associated with sudden, large jumps are avoided. Predictability, in many cases, may be the best way to guarantee regular income.

Any of these price-setting systems can be modified with a *capital-building* component. Charges are deliberately set a few percentage points above expected costs, and the surplus is invested to create a substantial cash reserve, available for emergencies or for funding major improvements. To be successful, this strategy requires careful long-term planning, and periods of high inflation may make it difficult, if not impossible, to carry out. On the other hand, it is the least painful and most economical way to finance improvements or restore a depleted reserve. For most condos (as opposed to co-ops) it may be absolutely imperative. (See "Borrowing," page 106, for an alternative open to co-ops and some other associations.)

Keep in mind that, as a general rule, *the higher the common charges, the lower the resale values,* and vice versa. When potential purchasers apply for mortgages, banks deduct the monthly charge from an applicant's income before computing the size of an "affordable" loan. Therefore, keeping maintenance charges under control also protects the value of unit owners' investments.

Here's an example of the relationship between common charges and resale value: Al and Betty Mason want to buy the Fergusons' two-bedroom condo. The Masons' combined income is $48,000 per year, or $4,000 a month. The bank figures they can allocate 37 percent of their pretax income (i.e., $1,480) to housing. If the monthly charge (including utilities) is $380, that leaves $1,100 for mortgage payments. At typical terms (10.5 percent for thirty years), this would cover a mortgage of $120,000. If the Masons have saved $30,000 for a down payment, they could afford to put 20 percent down and offer the Fergusons as much as

$150,000 for the condo. But if the common charge is $580 and all the other numbers remain the same, the bank will limit their mortgage to $98,000; even if the Masons use the same $30,000 in savings for a down payment, they could offer no more than $128,000 for the apartment.

The precise figures will vary, of course, depending on market conditions and individual circumstances, but it is always in the established owners' interest to keep the common charges as low as possible, consistent with maintaining a sufficient cash reserve and necessary building services.

Setting the charges artificially low, however, can also undermine the value of unit owners' investments. Buyers normally ask to see the association's recent financial statements, and if the figures show a persistent deficit, the prospective purchasers and their bankers are going to assume that an increase in common charges, a substantial special assessment, or both, lie in the immediate future, adjusting their offering prices accordingly. When reserve figures are disclosed—as the State of California, for example, requires—buyers and mortgage-issuers may also deduct any significant shortfall from their calculations of a fair price.

Collecting What's Owed You

No matter what level the charges are set at, they must be collected promptly. When arrears pile up, it becomes difficult to cover even essential operating expenses. Every board should have a clearly articulated and rigorously enforced policy on delinquencies. Imposing a late charge on payments more than fifteen days overdue and instituting legal action against any unit owner who falls sixty days behind is a common approach. While the right of the association to impose penalties is unquestioned, a simple vote of the board may not suffice to make it effective: State law or your governing documents may require an amendment to provide for a new charge. Depending on the rules of your association, you'll need at least a majority—and perhaps all—the unit owners to approve the change. Since a late-charge rule protects the conscientious majority against a careless minority, it should not be hard to gain support for the idea, though quite a bit of paperwork will likely be required. In some states, another problem may arise. Where the courts have determined that late charges are a form of interest, usury laws may limit the fee to an amount that's too low (1 or 2 percent of the monthly charge) to have any deterrent effect. For all these reasons, you should discuss your plans with your lawyer and choose the one that would be easiest and most effective for you. Even in a small association with a good record of solving problems on an informal basis, it's important to spell out money rules in black and white. The object is to be prepared for the crisis no one expects.

An alternative to a late charge, called *acceleration*, has become increasingly popular as a tool for encouraging prompt payments. This penalty relies on the fact that governing documents routinely define the maintenance charge as an annual sum, which the association allows members to pay on a monthly basis solely as an accommodation. Acceleration is simply the withdrawal of this accommodation: a demand that a full year's mantainence be paid immediately, in one lump sum. It is important to set a deadline for the unit owner and to send a letter formally declaring him or her "in default" under your regulations. Be sure to send a copy to the unit owner's mortgage-holder, as well.

The failure to act can lead to big trouble, as the Terrace Garden discovered. This condo's council was reluctant to press action against a neighbor they knew to be experiencing financial difficulty. But after five months of arrears piled up, their patience was exhausted, and they instructed their lawyer to begin collection actions. Unfortunately, the Internal Revenue Service, among other creditors, got to court first, and it was more than a year before the condo got its funds. In other words, the building had to operate for eighteen months with no revenue at all from one unit and income continually under budget. Today, not surprisingly, Terrace Garden makes no exceptions to its policy on delinquencies.

Special Assessments

Another option for raising money from members is a special assessment *in addition to* the regular monthly charge. The assessment can be in any amount, as long as it is apportioned according to each owner's relative share of the complex. If the condo's new central air conditioning unit costs $370,000, then a unit owner with .055 percent of the common elements would owe $203.50. If the new roof costs $80,000 and there are five hundred shares in the co-op, the assessment is $160 a share, and the owner of a thirty-share apartment must pay $4,800. The advantage of such a charge is obvious: The problem is solved in one stroke, without the delays and expense of borrowing. The disadvantage, just as clearly, is the necessity of asking each owner to come up with a substantial sum in a single payment.

In many cases, an assessment above a certain amount must be put to a vote of all association members. If the assessment is to win approval, the need must be clear and the budget credibly formulated.

The blow can be cushioned through various strategies. If the complex has a cash reserve, the board may offer financing terms to unit owners—typically permitting the assessment to be paid in equal installments over three, six, or twelve months at slightly below-market interest rates—while meeting immediate cash needs from the reserve. If the improvement being financed will take several months to complete, the assessment can be divided into installments timed to coincide with progress payments due to the contractor. A Philadelphia condominium deliberately extended renovation work on its elevators over two years in order to spread out the assessment and make it more manageable for unit owners.

Several considerations can influence a board's decision to impose an assessment. First should be the condition of the development: Can all the needed work be financed with funds held in reserve? If not, can all desired improvements be financed with an assessment owners can realistically afford over a short term? If the answer is "No," then deferring less urgent projects (or borrowing, if possible) is the only choice. Try to estimate *all* the work likely to be needed;

repeated assessments in a short period can stir resentment and create real hardship for owners. A Manhattan condo, for example, installed elaborate marble paneling and new furniture in the lobby, assessing owners nearly twice the monthly charge to pay for it. Two months later, the board discovered major problems with the main pipes that carry water to upper floors and announced an even larger assessment to pay for plumbing repairs. The owners were, unsurprisingly, incensed. Many resisted paying the second assessment, and the entire board was voted out of office.

The age, career, and family condition of individual owners may influence the decision as well. One four-family co-op, faced with a hefty bill for rewiring, found itself divided between two "old" owners (who had bought in at a highly favorable price and carried almost no long-term debt) and two "new" owners (who had bought in more recently, paying much higher prices and taking on massive mortgage obligations). The former favored an assessment, which they could easily pay from savings on hand, thereby saving the association the expense of paying interest. The latter preferred borrowing, which would create only a small increase in monthly charges. While finance charges would raise the total cost, the interest on the borrowed funds would be a tax deduction for each unit owner. Eventually, the owners compromised on a borrowing "threshhold": Expenses under the agreed sum would be financed with an assessment; higher sums would be financed with loans.

Borrowing

Co-operatives—and, in some cases, condos and planned developments—can borrow against the value of property held in the association's name to finance major capital improvements. This practice is often called an *underlying mortgage,* and, in areas where associations are structured to permit borrowing, it is a common form of financing. But arranging it is more complex, costly, and time-consuming than looking for a personal mortgage. Banks are often reluctant to make such loans for less than $1 million, making it extremely difficult for small associations to borrow. Just to find a willing lender, you may have to pay a broker or lawyer a finder's fee (often ½ percent of the loan). Closing costs are also much higher than on individual loans. One New York co-op paid more than $25,000 in fees to borrow $750,000. Add such fees to interest at rates that over the past decade have often exceeded 10 percent, and you can see that borrowing, whatever its advantages, is costly.

Another disadvantage is the risk incurred. Commercial loans are usually not self-liquidating like personal mortgages; a massive "balloon" payment is normally due at the end of a five- or ten-year period. Under normal circumstances, the association can simply refinance this sum at current rates at the end of the term, usually with the same bank. But a sudden jump in interest rates or a sharp decline in real estate values can make it difficult, expensive, or even impossible to refinance the full balance due. In such a case (rare, but not unprecedented), the owners might have to be assessed to pay the full amount due.

The offsetting advantage of an underlying mortgage is that all the interest is tax-deductible to the individual owners, on an apportioned basis. Although the total outlay may far exceed the cost of an assessment, the tax-adjusted expenses may be easier for individual owners to carry, since Uncle Sam picks up part of the burden. And when it comes to price impact, the higher the deductible expenses, the more attractive an apartment to high-earning buyers seeking tax shelters.

Borrowing offers one other advantage: It "liberates" the increased equity your property has accumulated, turning it into cash you can use to further enhance the development's value and improve the quality of life of its owners. Professional real estate managers, in fact, routinely mortgage all their holdings and consider unmortgaged property a wasted asset. Larger developments should consider judicious borrowing a routine financial-management technique. Closely monitoring financial markets may make it possible to refinance at lower interest costs or to raise a considerable amount of cash at only a modest increase in carrying charges. The risk remains, however, and so boards should approach borrowing with caution, especially in small buildings where the potential cost to individual owners can be substantial.

Cash Reserve

Every organization needs some money in the bank to cover unexpected expenses, and this reserve can be tapped for a variety of purposes—to finance capital improvements, to cover unexpected shortfalls, to provide a cushion for emergencies. Most shared-ownership developments start out with an "endowment" (usually called *initial reserve* or *working capital)* from the developer. Surpluses earned when costs come in under budget increase that amount. On the other hand, unexpectedly high costs or ambitious capital improvements can soon deplete this reserve.

How big a reserve is enough? A lot depends on the condition of your property. If no major repairs or improvements are needed, a reserve equal to as little as 25 percent of projected annual expenses may suffice, though some financial advisors recommend three times that amount. If major capital expenditures are anticipated—a new heating system, repaving roads, repointing masonry, new recreational facilities—the reserve should be built up systematically to provide as much of the necessary funds as possible.

Because the failure of a shared-interest development can have serious repercussions for all its owners, while an adequate reserve provides insurance against such a failure, many states have considered (though, at this writing, none has adopted) laws mandating specific minimums, depending on the size of the association. California has passed a disclosure law, requiring each association to draw up a reserve plan and report regularly to members on its implementation. This practice is a good one for all shared-ownership developments, whether or not it is mandated by law.

When a reserve falls below the recommended minimum, it should be replenished through increased maintenance charges or even a special assessment. If the balance grows substantially larger, though, the board should consider a reduction in carrying charges unless capital improvements are planned. This is a point on which unit owners should closely question board members. (For more information, see "How to Read a Financial Statement," page 152.)

Other Revenue Sources: Service Charges

If your complex has facilities beyond basic living quarters—a parking lot, a health spa, or storage lockers, for example—you can impose reasonable charges for their use, usually added to the monthly maintenance bill. The rates are usually set a bit lower than those imposed by commercial facilities in your area; if local garages charge $50 a month, $40 might be a fair parking fee for residents of your complex. These charges can also be a method for assigning resources in short supply. If your basement has only thirty storage lockers for fifty apartments, it's perfectly logical to assign them to the residents who are willing to pay for this additional privilege. It's also possible to spare yourself some administrative work by contracting such services out (see "Concessionaires," below.)

Service charges can also be imposed for "one-time" services: moving in or out, to cite a common example. A complex with a large staff may also want to offer services like painting, cleaning, or light carpentry, which are particularly popular in commercial condos. The additional work can make it easier to carry a large number of specialists on the payroll, and pricing can include a certain amount for overhead. Some cities and states limit the amounts that can be charged or restrict the circumstances under which charges can be imposed, so check with your lawyer about local regulations before taking action.

Late and Penalty Charges

As discussed above (see page 103), owners who pay late should be subject to charges which both penalize the offender and repay costs incurred by the condo. Some associations also impose fines for rules violations, particularly those that involve additional expenses to the association. For example, if a dog is allowed to run free, in defiance of a leash rule, it may damage the flowers or shrubbery. A fine would help cover the expense of the extra work required of the grounds crew.

Flip Taxes and Sublet Fees

A charge on owners who sublet or sell out for a quick profit can usually be imposed by the board of a shared-interest development, though there are restrictions in some areas; check with your lawyer before you act. A *flip tax* (or, more properly, a *resale fee)* is intended to capture for the development as a whole a portion of the profit unit owners make from propertywide improvements. The Summit, recently converted to condo status, assesses a $5,000 fee on a sale by an "insider" (a rental tenant who bought in at a special reduced price) and a flat 1 percent of the sale price in other cases. Flip taxes can also be scaled to discourage rapid turnover. The Newtown House, for example, charges 30 percent of the net profit earned by a seller in the development less than one year, 20 percent for two-year owners, 10 percent for three-year owners; longer-term owners pay no fee when they sell.

While a flip tax has considerable appeal, it also entails lots of headaches. One based on net profits is hard to administer unless there are reliable historical records. A flat fee falls more heavily on sellers of small units than on sellers of large ones. In a tight market, the fee may be passed along to buyers through increased prices. And if the board has not carefully built support among owners for the policy, it may face a legal challenge.

A sublet fee, imposed on owners who rent their units to outside tenants, is much less controversial, since it serves to discourage speculators from buying into the complex while encouraging the development of a stable community of owners. The fee can be a flat sum, imposed when the application to sublet is processed; a percentage of the rent paid by the subtenant; or a flat monthly surcharge on the maintenance bill. To avoid rancor and confusion, the board should announce its policy clearly in advance and enforce it uniformly. (See page 73 for more information on monitoring rentals and sales.)

Commercial Tenants

If your complex includes retail or office space, you probably earn substantial revenues by renting out these commercial premises. (Unless, of course, the original developer retained these spaces for himself or sold them separately!) There are some limits to keep in mind, though. Recent tax-law changes reduce potential earnings from commercial rentals, since the association must pay corporate taxes on all such revenues. Associations must also limit their income from "outside" sources to no more than 20 percent of total revenues in order to protect their special tax status. One building on a prime New York shopping street actually gave a storefront rent-free to a local thrift shop to keep commercial income under this ceiling. To avoid potentially serious problems and ensure maximum benefit to the association, therefore, always consult your lawyer and accountant before drawing up, let alone signing, any commercial leases.

   In addition to legal and financial considerations, there are obvious limits on the type of tenant suitable for a mostly residential complex. A lively nightclub, for example, may prove incompatible with residents' desire to sleep. A restaurant or food store may generate unpleasant odors. And professional apartments that do not have private entrances from the street can bring a steady stream of outsiders into otherwise private areas of the complex. Weighing these practical and financial considerations is essential to making sure that commercial rentals make a positive contribution to your association.

Concessionaires

Sometimes, you can actually improve services and bring in some extra cash by contracting with outside agencies to supply special services while paying the association for the privilege. The most common concession granted is a coin-operated laundry: An operating company supplies and services the machines, keeps the laundry room(s) clean, and collects the money, paying an agreed sum to the association each month. The size of the payment and the type of service are usually negotiable: A lower price-per-wash in return for a lower payment to the association, for example, or new equipment in return for a higher price-per-wash.

The possibility of establishing other concessions will depend on the physical facilities in your development. If you have a health club or garage, for example—or even space that could be developed into a health club or garage—you could bid out the operating contract to a concessionaire. The potential revenue to the association would depend on several factors: Are adequate physical facilities in place, or would the operator have to invest a substantial amount in building or updating them? Is the service restricted to residents or are outside users, paying premium rates, also acceptable? Does the board envision round-the-clock operation or limited hours? All these issues should be negotiated with potential bidders before a final decision is reached. It's also essential to discuss proposed contracts with your lawyer and accountant to be sure you don't inadvertently violate tax laws, zoning restrictions, or other regulations.

CONTROLLING ESSENTIAL EXPENSES

Insurance

In addition to the question of raising money for the development, there is the matter of protecting the owners' investment. Certain types of insurance are absolutely essential for any shared-ownership organization, and they are generally sold "bundled" in a comprehensive package:

1. *General liability insurance.* This type of insurance covers you whenever you are sued. If Mary McCarthy's nephew drives over a broken bottle in the parking lot and demands reimbursement for his damaged tires, if Mr. Stein's mother slips on the newly waxed floor and breaks her hip, if the burst pipe on the sixth floor ruins the Bergens' dining room carpet, this policy will cover any expense for which the association is liable. There is also a collateral benefit: In the event of a major lawsuit, the insurance company will take the responsibility and bear the expense of defending the case in court.

The problems, on the other hand, have made the front pages. In view of the record-breaking sums juries have been awarding victims of negligence, insurance companies have been raising premiums and lowering benefit ceilings. Your lawyer can give you an idea of typical settlements in your area, but do not be surprised if your present policy covers only a fraction of such sums. The rule of thumb is to buy as much coverage as the company offers and your budget permits. If the offered maximum coverage is ridiculously low (say $1 million or less), you may want to explore the possibility of joining a local association—perhaps organized by your managing agent—and buying part of an "umbrella" policy covering liability awards in excess of the basic insurance policy carried by the individual developments.

2. *Officers and directors insurance.* This is fundamentally an extension of your liability policy to the volunteer leaders of your association, protecting them from personal liability for any steps they take on behalf of the association. In most states, members of a board of directors can be sued both individually and collectively for actions that cause harm to another person, so this coverage is indispensable. In some states, the coverage is legally mandated. In any event, few rational people would serve on the board without such protection!

3. *Interruption of business coverage.* If six owners are burned out in a fire, they aren't going to pay common charges for the period they can't live in their units. But

most of the association's expenses (payroll, mortgage, insurance) will continue unabated, and you need even more cash to rebuild the damaged wing. This coverage reimburses you for the revenues lost through a covered hazard.

4. *"Non-owned car" insurance.* Mary Schmidt drove her station wagon to the nursery to pick up new plants for the garden. In the crowded parking lot, she dented another car's fender. Bill Dickson was driving home with a new light fixture for the lobby when he struck a neighbor's Doberman; the dog's owners are suing the condo among other defendants. It's in circumstances like these that this coverage comes into play. The need is admittedly rare, but the insurance is not expensive and seems to be inevitably included in comprehensive coverage.

5. *"All hazards" protection.* This protects all commonly held property—the entire structure of a high-rise as well as all shared areas in a town house development or planned community—in case of damage from fire, wind, or accident. Such policies explicitly exclude flood and earthquake damage; if either is a major hazard in your area, you'll have to consider buying additional coverage.

Because of the overlap between areas that are the responsibility of individual owners and the association's liability, it is highly advisable for unit owners to carry their own homeowner's insurance. In many developments, the board requires each unit owner to carry a minimum amount of insurance. In cities with many shared-interest developments, local insurance agents may be willing to give discount rates if several individual unit owners buy their policies at the same time. Agents may even approach the board and ask the association to formally endorse a specific company, in return for a discount to all purchasers. If the board, or one of its committees, has the time to investigate this offer and determine whether it is especially attractive, then the endorsement can be a real service to unit owners. On the other hand, if researching the offer requires time the board does not have, unit owners are probably better off shopping individually for policies that meet their particular needs.

Although specific details will vary, condo and co-op insurance coverage is likely to come in a package, on a take-it-or-leave-it basis. Like any other major purchase, insurance contracts for the entire complex should be awarded on the basis of competitive bidding. This need not be done every year, provided service remains satisfactory; it's always wise to avoid gaining a reputation as an "insurance hopper." But every three or four years, it's worth the effort to discover what your current carrier's competitors are offering. Small buildings, in particular, are likely to find a range of services and prices available. In evaluating options, a knowledgeable insurance agent can be an invaluable aid. Talk to agents who work with similar developments in your area and with those who provide business insurance to residents. Good insurance counsel can be as valuable as a good lawyer or accountant.

Taxes

The belief that "you can't fight City Hall" is an expensive misconception in many parts of the country. Errors in property tax bills and in property tax assessments are far more common than most people believe, and when the error occurs on a multiunit dwelling, the total cost can reach into the thousands, even millions, of dollars. For example, some cities reassess property only when it is sold. If your complex was recently converted to joint ownership, you could therefore face a much larger tax bill than a comparable complex that's still a rental. Overcharges also result when the tax law is misapplied, treating your complex as a commercial property instead of owner-occupied private residences; the latter are usually assessed at a lower percentage of their market value, taxed at lower rates, or both.

In any city, it's important to know where, when, and how to appeal an overcharge. You can try the local tax information number in the phone book, or ask the staff of the city council member or state legislator for your district to assist you. Your regular lawyer may be able to advise, or you may choose to hire a specialist on a contingency basis: You pay nothing unless the attorney reduces your taxes. In a co-op, the board or managing agent bears responsibility for overseeing tax matters. In a condo, each owner is personally responsible for taxes, but the owners association or agent can advise members and coordinate filings. In any event, both owners and the board should ensure that all channels of appeal are regularly utilized to avoid unnecessary tax expenditures.

Similarly, every multiowner development should be sure to investigate tax advantages that may be offered by city, state, or federal agencies for improvement work completed in your complex. If your building qualifies as "historic," you probably are eligible for an especially wide range of tax benefits, from the federal level on down, for any improvements classed as "preservation" or "restoration." If you are not certain of your status, check with your local historical society or landmark preservation commission. If you are in a "transitional" (or "gentrifying") neighborhood, your city may award special tax credits for improving a long-neglected structure. Some jurisdictions will grant reductions for major capital improvements: rebuilt elevators, new roof, replacement windows, etc. The rule of thumb: Check it out! Your managing agent, your neighbors, or your city council member should have more detailed information.

The same rule applies to any unexpected notice of "unpaid" taxes. If you have a mortgage, the bank usually pays these taxes from an escrow account and is unlikely (to put it mildly!) to skip a payment. Your first response on receiving such a notice, therefore, should be to call the bank's tax department and ask them to investigate. In a co-op with no underlying borrowing, call your managing agent, your lawyer, or the tax collector's office to get the matter straightened out. In any event, don't make any payments until you are satisfied the charge is legitimate.

And while property levies are the largest tax item, don't overlook other charges which may be incorrectly assessed against you. In Pennsylvania, for example, the state legislature repealed the sales tax on utility bills for private, owner-occupied residences. Most of the state's condos, however, did not immediately benefit. Following the local real estate custom, they had only one central meter for the entire building, including energy costs in the monthly carrying charge. The electric companies therefore classified them as "commercial" customers and, with the approval of the Public Utilities Commission, continued to assess sales tax at the maximum rate. A lawyer who sat on the board of a Philadelphia condo organized an ad hoc federation of condos across the state, took the matter to court, and eventually won not only removal of the sales tax from future power bills but also a rebate of all taxes collected since the repeal law took effect. His own building got a $70,000 credit.

Heartened by this victory, he's now taking on a similar problem. The city provides refuse collection from private homes as a municipal service, but commercial properties must pay a private carter to dispose of the trash. Condo owners, in effect, pay twice for sanitation services—their taxes, as private home-owners, plus trash-hauling fees. If the lawyer can convince the city to apply the same logic used in the power case, his building could save nearly $10,000 a year—and hundreds of other condos would benefit as well. The moral is clear: Make sure the taxing authorities recognize that your complex consists of private, residential properties, each entitled to the same privileges and services as a freestanding house.

Paying Contractors

There are tips on finding and dealing with contractors in the discussion of the board's responsibilities (see page 68). From a financial point of view, the key point to remember is simple: Don't pay until you're satisfied with what you've received. This may sound obvious, but it's not always easy to stick to. The contractor's expertise can be intimidating, and any disruption of the work soon creates pressures on the board and the manager to finish the job as quickly as possible. Paying up "just to get it done" becomes a potent, if not always logical, argument.

The place to start dealing with such pressures is in the contract itself. When "progress payments" are called for, conditions for payments should be clearly spelled out. For example, a replacement window contract might specify 25 percent on signing (to signal the board's serious intent and to provide some working capital for the contractor), 25 percent on delivery of materials to the building (the manager or a board member should verify these deliveries), 25 percent on "satisfactory completion" of half the work, and 25 percent on "satisfactory completion" of the entire project. If you are financing the project with special assessments on owners, you can also specify a timetable in the contract, so that you can match the timing of the assessment to the due dates of the installment payments. If you have hired a consulting engineer, "satisfactory completion" should be defined *in the contract* to specify *written approval* by the engineer. In other cases, "satisfactory completion" should be defined in clear and objective terms: For example, "fully operative windows and frames mounted in [number] units, including all mounting hardware and finish work." Before authorizing payment, of course, inspect to be sure the work has been completed to your specifications.

The proportion paid at each stage of the work will vary, depending on the nature of the project. As a general rule, try to make the final, "on-completion" payment as large as possible—*at least* 15 percent of the total contract—to maximize your influence in any dispute. Withholding progress payments can cause delays, since the contractor can always pull the workers off the job, freezing work and prolonging disruption. Once the work is substantially complete, however, the leverage is almost entirely on your side.

Don't be surprised if there are a few "extras" to pay for. Despite the best efforts of board, manager, and contractor, some legitimate unexpected expenses may arise. Garden Estates, for instance, hired Upson Downs Corporation to rebuild its elevators. The mechanical aspects of the job went well, but the doors Upson supplied were ugly and institutional. Custom doors, appropriate to the art deco style of the building's public areas, cost an additional $300 per floor, but the board chose to pay it in order to preserve the building's distinctive character. Some contracts will, in fact, come in precisely at the agreed sum, but it's always wise to factor into your budget 5 to 10 percent for overruns.

Occasionally the opposite case arises: A contractor is unable to meet your specifications and substitutes a less expensive alternative. Such a change may be grounds for revoking the contract, or it may be simply an inevitable compromise. Conway Court hired Glen Boskey Landscapers to redo the grounds, specifying a number of trees and other decorative plantings. But Glen Boskey was unable to furnish two of the relatively rare trees included in the plan. After much negotiation, Conway Court got an offsetting credit for garden supplies needed for the upkeep of their grounds.

Hamilton Towers was not so lucky. Midway through a repainting of the public areas, one of the board members noticed that the painters were using Penny-Pincher paint rather than the Dura-Cote specified in the contract. Confronting the contractor with his apparent deception, the board persuaded him to add two coats of Dura-Cote at no additional charge. They could have demanded a sharp reduction in the cost of the work actually done, but they would have still faced the necessity of hiring another painter to finish the job. And the total cost of even the discounted work done, plus the additional costs of a new contract, would doubtless have exceeded the sum originally budgeted.

Once a contract is signed, it's usually easier to deal with the company already on the job than to open negotiations with a new supplier. An important corollary: The time to ask "difficult" questions is *before* the contract is signed. Before providing your John Hancock, be sure you've agreed on all the terms.

Paying Routine Bills

If cash balances permit, you should make all payments due each month. In tight months, though, it may be necessary to establish priorities. A professional manager, if you have one, should handle this work for you. But if you handle the bills yourself, or if you want to check your manager's work, here's a system for ranking creditors:

1. *Mortgage and taxes.* Falling behind here risks the most dire consequences: losing the property.

2. *Payroll.* In many states, it's a felony to write a bad payroll check. More to the point, employees give better ser-

vice when they feel an employer is diligently taking care of obligations to the staff.

3. *Utilities, management service, and maintenance contracts.* These bills come around every month; ignoring them just makes them bigger and risks the loss of essential services.

4. *Heating fuel.* If you live in a cold climate, these bills will be substantial during the winter months. The gas or oil company may be willing to defer part of your payments or to establish a "level billing" program, involving regular monthly payments that smooth out high-season peaks. You'll probably have to begin such a plan early in the summer, so that a substantial credit builds up before the peak heating season. Small buildings will find it easier to make such arrangements, but most suppliers will be willing to consider any reasonable arrangement.

5. *Insurance.* As with heating costs, this large annual expense can usually be spread out over several months. Open negotiations by suggesting that the annual premium be spread over six equal monthly installments and see how your broker responds. Remember, though, that the broker's flexibility may be limited by the policies of the insurance carrier involved.

6. *Regular suppliers.* The local hardware store, the cleaning supplies company, the landscapers who maintain the garden—these bills can add up if unpaid. But the amounts are relatively small, and postponing payment occasionally will create few problems.

7. *Occasional suppliers.* The people you do not deal with every month can be asked to wait when you find yourself short of cash: The company that cleans the boiler each fall, the paint store you use once or twice a year, the pump repair company you call in an emergency, and similar suppliers.

8. *Professional services.* It is, in a sense, unfair to these skillful and highly trained people, but lawyers and accountants are traditionally the last to be paid. It's not that your obligation to them is any less; they should certainly be paid as quickly as possible. But they aren't carrying the large capital expenses of, say, a roofer, and they can't leave you in the dark, like the electric company. What's more, they

know your operations well and already have a pretty good idea of when they'll get paid.

SIGNING THE CHECKS

Who should sign checks for association expenses? If you employ an outside managing agent, it's customary and convenient to give signatory power over the operating fund to that company's top executives. As long as the agent provides a detailed monthly accounting, along with copies of paid bills and bank statements to verify them, there is little risk in this procedure. If the maintenance charge is set at a level close to actual expenses—the general rule—any irregularities will be quickly evident.

Control of reserve accounts is another matter. These figures often do not appear automatically on financial statements, and these funds should not be tapped, except for already planned capital expenditures or in case of an unforeseen cash shortage. Since these are circumstances of which the board must be aware, control of these accounts should sensibly rest with the board itself. Occasions on which the reserve must be tapped arise so seldom that leaving the minimal paperwork to the board is not usually burdensome. If you prefer to assign the bookkeeping tasks to the managing agent, make sure that at least one board member must sign any check or draft drawn on the reserve account. And, of course, be sure the reserve fund is kept in an interest-bearing account. Insist on seeing original documents for all transactions, including bank statements or passbooks and canceled checks; do not accept bland, unspecific assurances that "everything is under control." Reliable, professional managers welcome the opportunity to demonstrate their competence.

Much of this advice may seem obvious. And indeed, financial management of shared-ownership housing is mostly a matter of applied common sense. But it must be applied firmly, consistently, and with an eye on the telling details. To paraphrase an old adage, "Eternal vigilance is the price of solvency."

6
Key Documents:
Finding Answers in "The Book"

From the day you first make a serious offer on a unit, owning shared housing means confronting a mass of paperwork. The rules that govern the association and the reports that keep its members up to date come in a steady, sometimes overwhelming stream. It's easy to be intimidated by all these documents, if only because most of us aren't used to dealing firsthand with legal and financial papers.

Buried in the often dense verbiage, however, are rules governing your everyday life and the value of your investment. It's vital that you become familiar with the key documents that govern your association. This chapter will highlight the essential points and show how to find answers to common questions. Please remember that these comments are provided for general information only, to help explain the principles of shared-interest housing. The basic patterns are the same for all associations, but there is an almost infinite number of variations that can be worked on these themes. Local laws and customs, the specific needs of each particular development, even the personal style of the lawyer who draws up the papers make each condo, co-op, and planned community a unique institution. The documents for your complex will surely vary in some respects from these examples. When questions go beyond the broad outlines given here to the specific provisions of your charter, consult a knowledgeable local lawyer for the answers.

Keep in mind, too, the fact that these documents may contain flaws. Problems often arise from the way legal documents are drafted: A lawyer looks through a book of sample documents, picks those that seem to fit the current circumstances, and pastes them together, adding appropriate details. Unfortunately, these composite documents are seldom subject to a rigorous proofreading, and it remains to the hapless organizations that have to work with them to sort through any ambiguities and contradictions. If your development was only recently built or converted to shared ownership, it's likely you'll need to amend your regulations to correct errors. In addition, the experience of management by resident owners may reveal problems not considered by the sponsor in drawing up the original papers. For example, one New York co-op had by-laws requiring all board members to stand for reelection every year. As soon as the resident owners gained a majority, they adopted an amendment to permit staggered, two-year terms in order to gain more stability and continuity. Even if your documents have served you well for a number of years, you ought to examine them closely from time to time to see if they need updating.

THE BASIC CHARTER: ESTABLISHING AND DEFINING THE ASSOCIATION

The creation of a community association—condo, co-op, or homeowners association—requires two distinct but interrelated steps. First is the creation of a legal entity (which may be called an *association*, a *partnership*, a *corporation*, or something similar) to exercise the ultimate authority over all questions that touch on shared interests and to hold legal title to any jointly owned property. The document creating this entity is usually called a *declaration of condominium, covenant, prospectus*, or *charter;* if a corporation is involved, there will also be a *certificate of incorporation*. The rules governing the functioning of this organization (how leaders are chosen, how finances are regulated, how decisions are made by the membership, etc.)

are usually set out in a separate companion document, called the *code of regulations* or the *by-laws.*

Next comes the document that spells out in detail the rules governing relations between individual owners and the association. In a condo, it's usually included in the *code of regulations;* in the case of a co-op, these terms are in a separate document, the *Proprietary Lease.* This is *the single most important document* among your "condo papers." It will be long, dull, and highly detailed, but you *must* read it through carefully. It will spell out your rights and obligations as a unit owner, the penalties the association can exact if you fail to meet your obligations, and the protections you have against poor policy decisions or malfeasance by the association's governors. Any disputes that arise have to be settled within the limits of its terms, which are very difficult to alter or amend.

The development's "book," as it is often called, should also include recent financial statements and the current house rules (both discussed below). Additional materials that may be offered as matters of information or required by local law—such as an engineer's report on the condition of the development at the time it was converted to joint ownership or a description of the rights of rental tenants who choose not to buy their units—are important to a property undergoing conversion but have mainly historic interest for long-established associations.

On page 125 is the table of contents from a typical condominium's declaration, followed by comments on potentially obscure or important points. Specific terminology and format will vary from state to state, from city to city, and between co-ops and condos, but the issues addressed remain the same.

THE EXEMPLAR

Declaration of Condominium

TABLE OF CONTENTS

Submission of Property to Unit Property Act

This item simply refers to the law under which the condominum is organized. "Definitions," however, are complex and crucial. For openers, these clauses include *a definition of precisely what you own* and where your individual responsibility stops and starts. Here is some typical language:

> The title lines of each Apartment are situated as shown on the Declaration Plan and are described as follows:
>
> (a) The Apartment side surface of the masonry portion of such exterior and interior walls of the Building as are adjacent to such Apartment.
>
> (b) The Apartment side surface of the core of interior partitions of the Building which separate such Apartment from adjoining Apartments or Common Elements (including, by way of illustration and not limitation, corridors which are for common use).
>
> (c) The Apartment side surface of furring around structural steel columns, utility shafts, and other Common Elements within or passing through such Apartment.
>
> (d) The Apartment side surface of ceilings and furring under and around overhead structural steel members, utilities, and other structural steel members, utilities, and other Common Elements.
>
> (e) The Apartment side surface of the structural concrete floor of such Apartment.
>
> (f) The Apartment side surface of the sash windows which are set in the exterior walls of such Apartment, the exterior surface of the panes of such windows, and the Apartment side surface of window stools for such windows.
>
> (g) The exterior surface of doors, and their sills and hardware, between such Apartment and adjacent Common Elements (including by way of illustration and not limitation, corridors for common use), and the Apartment side surface of the door frames in which such doors are set.

These paragraphs establish the "boundaries" (or *title line*, as it's formally known) of an apartment. Since they include the surface of walls, ceilings, floors, and so forth, the phrase "from the paint out" is often used to describe the area of individual responsibility. Everything *behind* the paint—utility lines, structural supports, the walls themselves—is part of the Common Elements and is maintained by the association.

If you have trouble understanding the text, try studying it alongside the floor plan or while examining a door or window or whatever is being discussed. Take each sentence phrase by phrase, examining each specific item as it is named; you should then have both a verbal and a real-world picture of the issue. If this technique fails, ask your lawyer to "walk you through" a few confusing clauses until you get the hang of it. For example, after defining the title lines above, the declaration goes on to define what makes up an apartment:

(a) The air space enclosed within such title lines . . .

(b) All partitions which are wholly contained within such title lines, including all doors, door frames, hardware, electrical outlets and wiring, telephone outlets and conduits, and other items and devices in such partitions.

(c) Entrances into Apartments from the adjacent common corridor are shown on the Declaration Plan as openings in the corridor partitions. Each such opening is equipped with a door, door frame, sill, and hardware and, except for the door frames and the common corridor surface of such doors, sills, and hardware, all of the foregoing are within the title lines of such Apartment.

(d) All glass, including the interior and exterior surfaces thereof, which are set in sash in exterior walls of such Apartment. The window sash and window stool (except the Apartment side surface of the window sash and window stool) are Common Elements.

(e) All kitchen equipment, including their water, waste, gas and electrical connections, which are located within the title lines of such Apartment.

(f) Electrical lighting and power circuits serving only such Apartment (including, by way of illustration and not limitation, the wiring and all terminal devices, and the fuse or circuit breaker devices, even though the circuit breaker protective devices and the wiring to them are located outside the title lines of such Apartment).

If you look at the front door while reading item (c), you'll realize that you are responsible for everything about the door (including the locks), but the condo has the exclusive right to paint the corridor-side surface. This clause also means you can't hang a Christmas wreath or even a knocker on the door without the board's permission. In practice, a modest, tasteful decoration is unlikely to lead to a confrontation, although a determination to crack down on rule violations or complaints from other residents could lead to a request for you to remove the offending item. Item (d) means you pay for washing your own windows, replacing broken glass, and painting the inside of the window frame, but you can't replace the windows unilaterally, since the frame and sash belong to the condo association. And (f) makes you responsible for your fuse box and its wiring, even if it's outside your unit.

A Definition of "Commercial Space"

The "Definitions" section also explains the relationship between the residential association and any stores or offices on the property. In some cases, these units are sold on substantially the same terms as the apartments, with both commercial and residential owners belonging to the same association. This arrangement is particularly favorable to the residential owners, since they are certain to be a majority in the association. In large multiuse complexes, two completely separate legal entities—a residential condominium and a commercial condominium—may be set up within the same physical structure. In other buildings, the title to the commercial areas may be retained as an investment by the developer. Or the commercial space might be defined as part of the common areas, so that the association can rent it out on its own account.

Each of these arrangements has specific consequences—both good and bad—for the property's zoning, assessment, financial, and tax status. If your building has stores, offices, or other nonresidential units, discuss their status with your lawyer, accountant, or real estate professional to be sure you're maximizing the advantages and minimizing the risks.

A Definition with Flexibility

A well-drafted declaration will try to build some flexibility into its definitions, but it's not easy to do. For example:

> Whenever in this Declaration and the Declaration Plan a ti-tle line of an Apartment is described as being the exterior surface of a designated part of the Building, it is intended thereby, and it is hereby declared, (i) that the Board, acting on behalf of all Unit Owners, shall retain the right, exercis-able at the Board's option, to require the Owner of such Apartment to clean, maintain, repair, replace, and/or paint the same in accordance with instructions of the Board and at the expense of such Owner, although the Board may at its option elect to pay the cost of the same out of the Com-mon Expense fund, and (ii) that the same may not be re-placed, refinished, or altered by a Unit Owner without having obtained the prior written approval of the Board.
>
> Wherever in this Declaration and the Declaration Plan a title line of an Apartment is described as being the upper surface of the structural concrete floor, it is intended thereby, and it is hereby declared, that the owner of such Apartment shall have an easement for the purpose of affix-ing and removing carpet, parquet flooring, and other floor coverings . . .

In other words, the board reserves the right to require individual owners to maintain "condo" property (asking a shopkeeper to sweep the sidewalk in front of his store or an upper-floor resident to clean an empty bird's nest off her window sill, for instance) while granting owners the right to use "common" property to improve individual units (like changing the wiring or laying carpet). While all this verbi-age seems excessive, plans that overlook the details can cre-ate lots of headaches. The owner of a California town house, for example, discovered water in her basement, tracing the leak to a crack between the sidewalk and her exterior wall. A careful reading of the plan showed that she was respon-sible for the wall, the board was responsible for the walk, and no mention was made of the point at which they met! The matter had to be taken up at a special owner's meeting so that the plan could be amended.

Defining the Board

Basic qualifications for board members may be included among the "definitions." Usually, the clause will require that members be "natural individuals" (i.e., real, live people, rather than trusts, corporations, or other legal entities) and permit nonresidents to serve. In the early years of a development, permitting nonresidents to serve allows the sponsor's interests to be represented (see page 134). Once residents take full control of the property, they may want to drop it, though retaining the option has its advantages. You may want to put your managing agent on the board, a representative of the tenants council, if there is a large number of rental tenants, or even a lawyer or accountant, if you want to keep them more fully involved in your affairs.

Describing the Property

Sections 2, 3, and 4 of this declaration provide a precise description of the property involved. The declaration plan is the detailed site plan filed with the local recorder of deeds. It's rarely necessary for an individual owner to consult it or related documents, though these official records are often useful to the board in planning renovations or settling disputes with the city or neighbors.

Common Elements

This section allocates commonly owned parts of the building (hallways, utilities, storage areas, etc.) among individual owners, according to the relative size and value of their units. (In a co-op, a similar table is headed "Allocation of Shares.") Normally, this allocation is done entirely on the basis of size. If the total floor area of the property is 10,000 square feet, a unit of 900 square feet would get 0.9 percent of the "undivided common elements" in a condo or 0.9 percent of the total of all shares in a co-op. In some cases, however, the allocation reflects other factors that influence unit value. In an oceanfront development, for example, water-view units command a much higher price than land-view units; in a high-rise, upper floors command higher prices.

The allocation directly determines both the size of a unit's monthly maintenance bill and the vote each owner has in community affairs. While some condos have a "one owner, one vote" rule, proportional voting is much more common. In new developments or new conversions, errors sometimes occur in these allocations, particularly where setbacks, terraces, entrance lobbies, or other public areas change the "normal" size of a unit. Under such circumstances, it's worth comparing your unit with others of the same general size to make sure you're getting your fair share. Aside from obvious errors like this, it's almost impossible to change the allocation of shares; a unanimous vote of all unit owners is usually required.

Note also that each owner is required to support all common charges. The fact that you don't drive does not entitle you to a discount reflecting the cost of maintaining the garage, as long as parking is a service offered equally to all owners. Once you buy into a shared-ownership development, you are legally bound to accept *all* its rules and *all* its charges until you persuade fellow owners to change them formally, or until you sell your interest.

Easements

An *easement* is an agreement in which the owner of a specific piece of real property grants another person the right to use a portion of the property for a specified purpose. Since a condominium is divided among many property owners, easements are essential for the physical maintenance and operation of the property. An individual owner, for example, grants an easement to local utilities and the condo association to run water, steam, electric, and telephone lines through his or her unit to serve other units. The condo association grants an easement to owners who want to drive a nail into a commonly owned wall to hang a picture. In a co-op, on the other hand, there is only one property owner—the co-operative corporation—and easements are not necessary. The proprietary lease, however, will spell out conditions under which the co-op staff and management can enter individual units to perform maintenance and repairs.

Buried behind these legal niceties, however, is some very useful and important information: a detailed description of the kinds of routine work you can undertake without advance approval from the board, like laying carpet. In the interests of security, though, you should notify the staff or manager if you're going to have outside workers in your unit. At the same time, some easements may be conditional and incorporate restrictions. An easement granting unit owners access to the pool and patio, for example, may limit hours of use, forbid barbecues, and restrict guest privileges. These regulations may also be included in the house rules, though the ones included in the declaration carry more force and are much more difficult to change.

Purposes and Uses

These might also be called "restrictions," since this section spells out some strict limitations on the use of each unit. These rules are not likely to interfere with normal residential use of your home—indeed, they help protect your peace and your investment—but you should study them closely. Here's some typical language you're likely to encounter:

A. Except as hereinafter otherwise provided, Apartments may be used only for residential purposes and such professional purposes as shall be lawful and shall have been approved by the Board. . . .

B. The following additional restrictions shall apply to the use of all Units, subject to such rules and regulations regarding the scope and operation of the Units as shall be duly adopted from time to time under the Act or the Code of Regulations:

(i) No Unit Owner may obstruct the Common Elements in any way. No Unit Owner may store anything in or on the Common Elements without the prior consent of the Board.

(ii) The Common Elements shall be used only for the purpose for which they are intended and for the enjoyment of the occupants of all Units. No Unit Owner may carry on or practice, or permit any practice to be carried on, which unreasonably interferes with the quiet enjoyment by the occupants of any other Apartment or such Apartment, or any of them. The Property is to be maintained in a clean and sanitary condition. . . .

(iii) No Apartment shall be used, occupied, or kept in a manner which will in any way increase the fire insurance premiums for the Property, without the prior written permission of the Board, which permission may be conditioned upon the Unit Owner being required to bear the full amount of such increase. No Apartment or any part of the Common Elements shall be used, occupied, or kept in a manner which would violate any law, statute, ordinance, or regulation of any governmental body or which would lead to the cancellation of any hazard insurance policy on the Property. . . .

Clearly, the point here is to ensure that units are used only for legal, residential purposes that do not create unnecessary risks or impose an unfair burden on other unit owners. Note that section A requires advance board approval for *any* nonresidential use, even something legal and nondisruptive like writing or editing. And the insurance clause in paragraph (iii) could even come into play with certain hobbies whose materials present a perceived fire risk, like the chemicals used in photo processing or a kiln used for firing pottery.

The section likely to go on for dozens of paragraphs, covers matters as small as the kind of signs allowed on doors and as large as the conditions for joining two adjacent units into one larger apartment. The major point in the latter case is that the unit owner, rather than the association, must take responsibility for obtaining and paying for all official permits, inspections, and certificates. This stipulation is nearly universal.

Finally, here's a paragraph that rewards close reading:

No animals of any kind shall be raised, bred, or kept in any Apartment or Commercial Area; provided, however, that household pets may be raised, bred, or kept in any unit if permitted by the Board and if the Owner of such pet shall fully comply with any requirements imposed by the Board relating thereto.

The first words are "no animals," yet this paragraph actually empowers the board to *permit* pets in the building. As a general rule, avoid jumping to conclusions!

Initial Council Members

Except for buyers in the very early stages of a development's history, this section is of purely historical interest. The men and women named here are invariably business associates of the sponsor. It's doubtful any of them live on the premises; they may never even have seen the property!

Code of Regulations

This section gives the authority of the declaration to the house rules and the code of regulations. Every charter will have a similar provision in order to make those rules part of the basic agreement among unit owners and to give the board the power to enforce them with the same tools that can be used to enforce the charter itself—including, ultimately, default, foreclosure, and eviction. It's unlikely that a board would take such steps over, say, the wrong-size nameplate on the door, but unit owners should be aware that such rules do carry a lot of weight.

In case of conflict among provisions in the various documents, the declaration (or prospectus) generally takes precedence over the code of regulations (or by-laws or proprietary lease), which in turn takes precedence over the house rules. In other words, if anything in the regulations or house rules contradicts the declaration, the wording of the declaration applies.

Amendment of Declaration and Declaration Plan

Because the charter is the essential foundation of the condo or co-op, it is deliberately difficult to amend; the terms of so basic an agreement should not be changed without careful and deliberate consideration. Usually, a "super majority" of 75 or 80 percent of votes (remember that votes are weighted in most associations) is necessary for any amendment; some charters even require complete unanimity.

In addition, there are usually additional provisions for special situations. One might provide that no amendments affecting the sponsor's interest can be adopted without his or her concurrence. This would apply only during the conversion process, but where rental tenants are allowed to stay on indefinitely—and some states and cities make this their legal right—the "conversion process" can go on for decades.

Another common provision concerns the allocation of common elements (in a condo) or shares (in a co-op). Normally, there can be no changes in this allocation without the concurrence of all unit owners, or at least all unit owners directly affected. In practice, this makes it virtually impossible to change the allocation. The owner of a Manhattan penthouse, for example, was furious when a new building next door cut off his spectacular view. Because the value of his apartment was significantly reduced, he demanded a reallocation of shares. His neighbors were sympathetic—many of them had lost views, too—but saw no reason why *their* maintenance should be increased to compensate him. After all, the "damage" was done by a third party, and, more significantly, nothing in the co-op's documents guaranteed, or could have guaranteed, the view. There was no reallocation.

Removal of Property from Act

This section (which may also be headed "Dissolution") tells what happens if and when the property ceases to be jointly owned. In the case of a voluntary change in status, it's likely to require unanimous consent of all unit owners and assures that any profits are divided proportionally among them. An involuntary reversion to rental status, while unusual, is also possible. This situation most commonly arises when a property with an underlying mortgage defaults on the loan. Should this happen, owners are usually allowed to remain in residence as rental tenants of the bank, though they lose all their equity while remaining responsible for the outstanding balance of their personal mortgages. To head off such a catastrophe, the holder of the underlying mortgage may be willing to renegotiate the terms of the loan, provided new management is installed and a realistic financial plan is drawn up. This happened to several developments in the Northeast in late 1989, when a downturn in the real estate market left some highly leveraged sponsors unable to cover their financial obligations. Most of the resident boards were able to work out terms to save the owners' investments, but common charges shot up, and some services were reduced to cover the increased debt service. In rough times, then, both board members and unit owners should study this section to understand the risks of mismanagement.

Some Important Technicalities

Section 11 requires all buyers to accept the terms of the charter and the regulations; in the case of a condo, this section will usually specify that language to this effect must be included in the unit's deed. Sections 13 and 17 deal with getting the condo started, while section 14 provides for a "liberal interpretation" of the document (*e.g.*, overlooking obvious errors) and may also specify the law or laws under which disputes are to be settled. Section 15 concerns mortgages on the building at the time of conversion. In a condo, these are paid off as the units are sold; in a co-op, they become obligations of the co-operative corporation. And the "severability" of section 16 has nothing to do with relations among members of the association. It simply states that, if any part of the charter becomes illegal, the rest of the agreement will remain in full force. This legal "circuit breaker" ensures that if, say, a court declares your no-children rule discriminatory, the board will retain its authority to sign contracts and pay bills.

THE REGULATIONS (BY-LAWS AND PROPRIETARY LEASE): LAYING DOWN THE GROUND RULES

The next document, usually delivered in the same binder as the charter, is the set of rules governing the functioning of the association, typically called the *code of regulations* or *regulations and restrictions*. In a co-op these provisions are divided between two documents: the *by-laws*, describing the functioning of the co-operative corporation (officers, voting, powers, etc.), and the *proprietary lease*, which defines relations between the corporation and its tenant-shareholders. On pages 138–141 is a table of contents for the regulations that accompanied the declaration discussed above, with some commentary on the key points. You'll note a lot of overlapping, which is deliberate; well-drafted documents should reinforce each other. Most of the terms are self-explanatory, and if your own regulations have an equally detailed table of contents or index, you should find the answers to your questions quite easily.

Board members should study their development's rules carefully and consult them both before each owners meeting and before undertaking any major commitment. Unit owners who wish to question or challenge any board actions should study the rules, too, to make sure their objections are properly framed and presented. In extreme cases, unit owners have the right (spelled out under "Special Meetings") to demand a meeting to discuss an important issue or even to remove board members who have lost their confidence.

THE EXEMPLAR

Code of Regulations

TABLE OF CONTENTS

11. Miscellaneous
    A. Audits
    B. No Waiver
    C. Interpretation
    D. Personal Property
    E. No Partition
    F. Consent
    G. Amendment
    H. Severability
    I. Effective Date

Definitions

These should be exactly the same as those in the accompanying Declaration.

Owners Association

Membership

The rules here make it mandatory for all unit owners to join the association and for all members of the association to be unit owners. Similar language in co-op documents ties ownership of a specific block of shares to occupancy of a specific unit.

Meetings

Annual Meetings. All regulations and by-laws require at least one membership meeting a year, usually specifying a day (e.g., "the third Wednesday in May") with the qualifier "or such other time as the board may determine." While it's not necessary to stick to the designated date, regularity and consistency are important in building and maintaining member involvement, so meetings should be held, whenever possible, on the same date and in the same place each year. If there are no adequate meeting facilities on the premises, a nearby church or community center can probably make a room available for a modest rental. For the annual meeting, the by-laws often spell out two pieces of mandatory business—a financial report and election of board members—but a well-run meeting should give members a comprehensive view of the state of the property. See page 59 for additional ideas on organizing an owners meeting.

Special Meetings. In addition to the regular annual meeting, special meetings are called most often to discuss a major capital improvement or similar large-scale undertaking. These meetings are usually called by the board, but most regulations also establish a mechanism to permit the unit owners to call a meeting on their own, normally by getting a certain number of signatures (from, perhaps, 40 percent of the owners) on a petition. In any event, it is vital for the organizers to check the provisions under "Notice," which tell precisely how members are to be informed of special meetings and often limit the kind of business that can be conducted at them. Failing to meet the notice requirements could make it impossible to conduct official business at the meeting.

Quorum

To keep a determined minority from dominating association affairs, the regulations require that a minimum number of owners be present before official business can be conducted; owners holding an absolute majority of the proportional interests usually constitute a quorum. This safeguard is sensible, but many associations find it difficult to muster a quorum at some meetings. Ironically, associations split by divisions and troubled by serious problems are more likely to have good attendance than those that run smoothly. In any event, it's useful to have some sort of "circuit-breaker" clause to keep the association from being paralyzed by indifference. Here's a solution many associations adopt:

> Except as otherwise expressly provided in these Regulations, a quorum for all meetings shall exist if there is present, in person or by proxy, Unit Owners entitled to cast in excess of 50% of the votes of all members of the Association. If a quorum is not present at any meeting, the Unit Owners present may reschedule the meeting for a later date

and shall give all Unit Owners notice thereof in accordance with the provisions of these Regulations. If no quorum is present at such second meeting, the notice procedure shall be repeated if the Unit Owners present decide to call a third meeting. A quorum at such third meetings shall consist of whatever number of Unit Owners is present, whether or not their combined votes are in excess of fifty percent (50%) of the votes of all members of the Association.

The "three-strikes-you're-out" provision gives members two chances to be heard, then strips the lazy or indifferent of their votes to permit business to go forward. If your regulations contain similar language, it's a good idea to remind association members of it on each call to meeting, with a sentence like, "If you fail to attend or submit a proxy, you could lose your right to vote on these issues." If you would like to add this kind of clause to your regulations, ask your lawyer to draft it, to ensure that it complies with all local regulations and actually accomplishes what you want to accomplish.

Voting

The general rule is that voting is proportional to each unit owner's holdings, defined as "proportion of the undivided common interest" in condos and "shares" in co-ops; the allocation is determined in the declaration or prospectus (see page 130).

Proxies. To deal with the quorum problems mentioned above and to allow members who are unavoidably absent to have input in association affairs, proxies are usually permitted. The absent member simply designates someone who will be present to vote on his or her behalf. A proxy can be broad: Jack Brown can empower Mary Baldwin, with whom he usually agrees on association affairs, to speak on his behalf and cast his votes, as well as her own, on any matters that come before the meeting. Or proxies can be tied to very specific instructions. To ensure that all members can vote on new board members, for example, the outgoing board can distribute ballots and proxy forms. These proxies instruct an individual, typically one of the present officers, to cast the absent owner's ballot in the board elections according to the instructions written on the ballot. These highly specific proxies do not convey any other powers to their holders.

To prevent abuse, the regulations will likely impose certain restictions: Proxies must be in writing, must be announced and presented to the secretary at the beginning of the meeting, and must be limited to one specifically named meeting. If proxies become a troublesome issue at your association's meetings, you can refer to *Robert's Rules of Order* or a similar authority on parliamentary procedure to resolve the dispute.

Cumulative Voting. This is a special process used to elect board members in developments undergoing conversion from rental status. Especially in cities and states with tenant-protection laws, this process can go on for decades, and this type of voting ensures that both resident owners and the sponsor have fair representation on the board. Here's how it works: Each unit owner has a total "pool" of votes equal to his or her normal proportional figure multiplied by the number of seats being filled. For example, in an election where five seats are at stake, the owner of a 32-vote unit would have a total of 160 (5 × 32) votes to cast. He or she could vote all 160 for a single candidate, split them 110/50 between two candidates, 40 apiece for four candidates, or any other combination he or she chooses. Since the sponsor is sure to concentrate all his votes on his proportion of the available seats, the resident owners should do likewise. If the sponsor holds, say, 40 percent of the voting power and the board has five members, the developer will cast all his votes for just two candidates, assuring their election and his own control of 40 percent of the board. Shareholders should similarly concentrate their votes on no more than three candidates to ensure that 60 percent of the seats are occupied by members of their choice.

Actions of Association Without a Meeting

Here's the ultimate solution to the problem of getting a large number of people in the same place at the same time: Don't even try. If the issue at hand can be clearly and concisely stated and resolved by a straightforward vote of the membership—for instance, the approval of a special assessment or an amendment to the regulations to permit staggered terms for board members—then it's likely the question can be settled by an exchange of written documents without the hassles of organizing a formal meeting. These "meetings on paper" are particularly popular in commercial condos, where busy executives don't have a lot of time for extra meetings, but any association can use them, in appropriate cases. This section should lay down the ground rules: What information needs to be supplied, how long each unit owner has to reply, and what mechanism can be used to override the process if owners find it unsatisfactory.

The Board, Officers, and Responsibilities

This portion of the regulations provides the framework for the governing board's organization and operations, issues discussed at length in Chapter 3. Two special provisions, however, deserve the attention of all association members: *resignations and removals* and *filling vacancies.*

It is, alas, an all-too-common experience for one or more board members to find that an unforeseen change in their personal or professional lives makes it impossible to continue in office; the regulations usually permit them to withdraw promptly and gracefully by submitting a letter of resignation to their fellow members. More rarely, a board member will prove so incompetent or so corrupt that he or she must be removed, either by the board itself or by the general membership; the mechanism for doing so will be spelled out in this section of the regulations.

When it comes to filling any vacancies, there are two methods generally in use. Some regulations require a vote by the full membership, a system that is more democratic but also cumbersome and time-consuming. If there are only a few months remaining in the term of the former board member, it may be easier to simply carry on short-handed until the next elections. Other regulations permit the remaining board members—even if they do not constitute a quorum of the original board—to choose whomever they wish to fill out the unexpired term or terms. This system is swift and efficient, ensuring that the board will almost always be at full strength, but it sacrifices a degree of owner involvement in the governing process.

Rights and Obligations of the Unit Owners

This is the most important section of the regulations. *If you read nothing else, you must study this section closely.* (This section corresponds to a co-op's proprietary lease.) Here are the rules governing the financial affairs of the association, spelled out in great detail, as well as the mechanism for settling disputes between individual owners and the association. There's a clear, detailed definition of "default" and a detailed list of the steps the board can take against owners who default on their obligations, financial and otherwise, to the association. (For further information on financial questions, see Chapter 5.)

Often overlooked is the "doomsday" scenario (here, section E) explaining an owner's rights and the association's obligations in the event of the complete destruction of all or part of the development. While the possibility may seem remote, owners should discuss these provisions with their lawyers and insurance agents to be sure their interests are adequately protected, especially in regions at risk of major disasters like earthquakes, floods, or hurricanes. These provisions may also come into play in neighborhoods undergoing rapid development or redevelopment. Careless construction on adjacent sites can cause major, even disastrous damage to the condo. Or the developer of your complex might decide, for example, to put a couple of extra stories on a low-rise building, or to construct twenty new town houses in the middle of an expansive lawn; the reconstruction provisions could determine what voice the residents have in these changes and what compensation, if any, they would receive.

It is essential that board members and unit owners alike understand the terms of these rights and obligations (or of the proprietary lease) and stick to them, first, to minimize legal hassles if a problem arises and, more important, to avoid misunderstandings and resolve disputes quickly and equitably.

"Nonliability of Management"

This phrase sounds like a dodge, but these restrictions are essential to assure that you can find a board and a managing agent. If these individuals could be held personally liable for actions taken in good faith on behalf of the condo, they would probably find the risks too great to bear and refuse to serve. This section also defines the specific procedures used to sue the condo.

Insurance

Though it is not always spelled out in the basic documents, every shared-interest community needs insurance. The usual rule is that the association ensures the common areas—meaning the entire structure, in the case of an apartment building—but not the contents of any unit or even any structural elements defined as part of an individual unit, like the walls in a town house development. (See page 112 for more details.) Unit owners must purchase individual homeowner's policies to cover their units and their personal property; some condos, in fact, adopt rules requiring owners to do so. Whether it's a formal requirement or not, adequate coverage is essential, so make sure you have it!

Mortgages

In shared-ownership housing, there are three parties to every mortgage agreement: the unit owner, the bank or mortgage company, and the association. Both the mortgage holder and the association stand to lose if owners fail to live up to their obligations, so they agree to work together under the terms of an addendum to the mortgage papers, often called a *recognition agreement*. Each side agrees to recognize the other's interest in the unit: The association agrees to notify the bank if the owner defaults (for example, by falling behind in maintenance payments), and the bank agrees to notify the association if it is planning to foreclose on the mortgage note. While there are many local variations, the bank usually takes the lead in case of foreclosure, paying the association any overdue maintenance and selling the unit (subject to normal approval procedures) in order to recover the amount loaned.

In terms of personal budgeting, this means owners must give the *same priority* to monthly maintenance payments as to monthly mortgage payments. A failure to make either payment promptly and regularly can cost you your home and your equity.

Sections 10 and 11 tend to an assortment of small but useful legal points, just as similar parts of the declaration did. The procedures for amending the regulations may or may not be different from those for amending a condo declaration. In a co-op, the corporate by-laws are usually easier to amend (a simple majority vote of the shareholders may suffice) than the basic prospectus, though the terms of the propriety lease are virtually impossible to change, requiring unanimous assent.

HOUSE RULES: THE BASIS FOR A SMOOTHLY RUNNING COMMUNITY

House rules, sometimes called *community regulations*, might best be described as "institutionalized good manners." They simply spell out an agreed method of maintaining order and neighborliness in the development. But as explained earlier (page 134), these rules do have considerable force. Since the power to issue them is established in the development's basic documents, the power to enforce them is the same as it would be for such violations as defaulting on maintenance payments.

The accompanying sample covers a typical range of concerns. It's from a co-operative building, in which owners technically rent their units from the corporation they jointly own. For this reason, shareholders are called *lessees* and the co-operative corporation is the *lessor*. In a condo, the corresponding terms would be *unit owner* and *association*.

House Rules
The Bramwell Co-operative

1. The public areas of the building and grounds shall not be obstructed or used for any purpose other than ingress to and egress from the apartments in the building.

2. Children shall not play in the public areas and shall not be permitted on the roof, except for the child or guest of a Lesee who has exclusive use of a roof deck or terrace.

3. No public area shall be decorated or furnished by any Lessee in any manner without the prior consent of all of the Lessees to whose apartment such area serves as a means of ingress and egress; in the event of disagreement among such Lessees, the Board of Directors shall decide.

4. No Lessee shall make or permit any disturbing noises in the building or do or permit anything to be done therein which will interfere with the rights, comfort, or convenience of other Lessees. No Lessee shall play upon or suffer to be played upon any musical instrument or permit to be operated a phonograph or a radio or television loudspeaker in said Lessee's apartment between the hours of 11:00 PM and the following 8:00 AM if the same shall disturb or annoy other occupants of the building. No construction or repair work or other installation involving noise shall be conducted in any apartment except on weekdays (not including legal holidays) and only between the hours of 8:30 AM and 5:00 PM.

5. No article shall be placed in the public areas nor shall anything be hung or shaken from the doors and windows, or placed upon the window sills of the building.

6. No awnings or ventilators shall be used in or about the building except such as shall have been expressly approved by the Lessor or the Managing Agent, nor shall anything be projected out of any window of the building without similar approval, except air conditioning units.

7. No sign, notice, advertisement, or illumination shall be inscribed or exposed on or at any window or other part of the building, except such as shall have been approved in writing by the Lessor or the Managing Agent.

8. No bicycles, scooters, or similar vehicles shall be allowed to stand in the public areas.

9. Garbage and refuse from the apartments shall be disposed of only at such times and in such manner as the Superintendent, Lessor, or the Managing Agent of the building may direct.

10. Water closets and other water apparatus in the building shall not be used for any purposes other than those for which they were constructed, nor shall any sweepings, rubbish, rugs, or any other article be thrown into the water closets. The cost of repairing any damage resulting from misuse of any water closets or other apparatus shall be paid for by the Lessee in whose apartment it shall have been caused.

11. No Lessee shall send any employee of the Lessor out of the building on any private business of a Lessee.

12. Lessees may keep cats, dogs, or birds in the building without the permission of the Lessor so long as the keeping of such pets does not interfere with the rights or convenience of other Lessees. In no event shall dogs be permitted in any of the public portions of the building unless carried or on a leash. No pigeons or other birds or animals shall be fed from the window sills, terraces, balconies, or in the yard, court spaces, or other public portions of the building, or on the sidewalk or street adjacent to the building.

13. No radio or television aerial shall be attached to or hung from the exterior of the building without the prior written approval of the Lessor or the Managing Agent.

14. Unless expressly authorized by the Board of Directors in each case, the floors of each apartment must be covered with rugs or

carpeting or equally effective noise-reducing material, to the extent of at least 50% of the floor area of each room excepting only kitchens, pantries, bathrooms, maid's rooms, closets, and foyers.

15. No group tour or exhibition of any apartment or its contents shall be conducted, nor shall any auction sale be held in any apartment without the consent of the Lessor or Managing Agent.

16. The Lessee shall keep the windows of the apartment clean. In case of refusal or neglect of the Lessee during ten days after notice in writing from the Lessor or the Managing Agent to clean the windows, such cleaning may be done by the Lessor, which shall have the right, by its officers or authorized agents, to enter the apartment for the purpose and to charge the cost of such cleaning to the Lessee.

17. Complaints regarding the service of the building shall be made in writing to the Board of Directors of the Lessor.

18. Any consent or approval given under these House Rules by the Lessor shall be revocable at any time.

19. The agents of the Lessor, and any contractor or workman authorized by the Lessor, may enter any apartment at any reasonable hour of the day for the purpose of inspecting such apartment to ascertain whether measures are necessary or desirable to control or exterminate any vermin, insects, or other pests and for the purpose of taking such measures as may be necessary to control or exterminate any such vermin, insects, or other pests. If the Lessor takes measures to control or exterminate carpet beetles, the cost thereof shall be payable by Lessee.

20. These House Rules may be added to, amended, or repealed at any time by resolution of the Board of Directors.

The rules fall into three overlapping categories. The largest group (1, 2, 6, 8, 9, 10, 11, 13, 16, 17, 18, and 19) defines steps necessary to ensure the safe and efficient operation of the building. Some of these rules (such as those concerning obstructions in the hallways and projections from the windows) are required by fire codes and insurance companies to avoid unnecessary risks.

The next group (1, 3, 5, 6, 7, 8, 9, 12, 13, 15, 16) speaks to matters of public order and appearance. Generally speaking, the more distinctive the appearance of the development and the more resale prices depend on the style and "tone" of the community, the more stringent such rules are likely to be, and the more strictly they must be enforced to protect those intangible values. Some planned communities go as far as limiting the colors that can be used for exterior painting, or requiring that curtains hung in windows visible from the street be of a specified style and color.

Finally, 1, 2, 3, 4, 12, 14, and 15 deal with questions concerning the relations among individual residents. The goal is simply to remove or reduce areas of potential conflict. Ideally, these rules are self-enforcing, through the residents' goodwill and their respect for one another's interests.

Note that in some cases—rule 3, for example—the definition of ambiguous terms and the enforcement of the rule is left to the residents themselves. Even the noise rule (4) imposes time limits only on those activities which "disturb or annoy other occupants." If the building is full of "party animals" who all boogie until 4:00 AM, there's no violation of the rule! This flexibility reflects a fundamental fact about shared-ownership developments: They are as staid or as lively, as elegant or as casual, as the residents want them to be. It's important for buyers to choose a development that suits their life-style and for boards to make rules that fit the buyers. Rule 20 permits amendment by a simple vote of the board, so these rules can be easily adapted to the needs and desires of the residents, both present and future.

HOW TO READ A FINANCIAL STATEMENT

By law, co-op and condominium associations are required to submit audited financial statements to their members on a regular basis—usually once a year. The importance of these numbers is clear, but they are, alas, presented in a form virtually unintelligible to the nonspecialist. Your accountant does not present these puzzling figures merely to annoy or confuse you; the profession has developed certain standards to which all financial reports must adhere. Because of these standards, for example, you can change accountants and be confident in comparing statements from year to year. Even more significantly, you can be sure the figures accurately represent your financial activities in a form acceptable to the IRS and other government agencies that regulate your activities.

On page 154 is a sample report, with explanatory footnotes added. (On pages 164–165, "Notes to Financial Statements," there are also notes, identified with Roman numerals, that were written by the accountants as part of the original report.) This is a co-op report, which is somewhat more complex than a typical condo report, particularly since condo associations do not usually have underlying mortgages to worry about. Depending on the specific legal structure of the association, there may also be a few differences in the terms used: "Fund Balance," for instance, instead of "Stockholders' Equity." Your treasurer or accountant should be able to clarify any specific items on *your* financial report that do not fall into these general categories.

THE PINES OWNERS ASSOCIATION, INC.
Statement of Assets, Liabilities, and Stockholders' Equity
December 31, 1989

ASSETS

Current Assets

Cash: checking account	$ 4,499
Cash: money market accounts	246,322
Accounts receivable ❶	5,382
Prepaid expenses ❷	9,708
TOTAL CURRENT ASSETS:	265,911

Restricted Deposits and Funded Reserves

Escrow accounts ❸	60,321

Property and Equipment ❹

Land	61,689
Building	702,379
Equipment	1,335
Boiler	40,000
	805,403
Less accumulated depreciation	(267,657)
Net property and equipment	537,746

Other Assets

Deferred mortgage costs ❺	23,333
TOTAL ASSETS:	887,311

LIABILITIES AND STOCKHOLDERS' EQUITY

Current Liabilities

Accounts payable and accrued expenses ❻	$41,436
Corporate taxes payable	6,281
Current portion of mortgage payable ❼	8,027
TOTAL CURRENT LIABILITIES:	55,744
Mortgage payable, net of current portion ❽	733,564
TOTAL LIABILITIES:	789,308

Stockholders' Equity ❾

Capital stock, $1 par value, 3,497 shares issued and outstanding	$3,497

Additional paid-in capital   180,623

Retained earnings (losses)   (86,117)

TOTAL STOCKHOLDERS' EQUITY: 98,003

TOTAL LIABILITIES AND STOCKHOLDERS' EQUITY:

$887,311

See accompanying notes to the financial statements.

What It Means

Statement of Assets, Liabilities, and Stockholders' Equity (Balance Sheet)

This is a "snapshot" of the association's financial status on the given date. In accordance with accounting conventions, it mixes very real money, like cash in the bank, with abstract expenses, like depreciation, and arbitrarily assigned values, including the "par value" of stock. Some of these numbers reflect your tax status; others are part of the accountants' checks on the accuracy and completeness of your records. The most important numbers on this page are the *total current assets* and *total current liabilities*. These figures indicate whether you have the means to pay your current bills, and whether any cash surplus is available for emergencies or improvements. Here are the explanatory notes (refer to reference numbers):

1. Money owed to you: typically, arrears on maintenance payments.

2. Money already paid out, but not due until some future date: In this case, The Pines had a property tax due January 1, so the check was sent in December. (It's odd to see money paid out listed as an *asset*, but the term is used because such payments can be applied against future liabilities.)

3. Money held in your name, but available only for a specified purpose: In this case, as in any building with an underlying mortgage, it's money collected from the building by the mortgage-holding bank to pay property taxes.

4. The value of your property for accounting and corporate tax purposes: normally the actual cost at the time the development was built or converted to joint ownership. This value is reduced by depreciation, according to a formula explained in the attached notes. Land is always listed separately, since it cannot be depreciated. Be careful not to confuse this "book value" of your property with two other, quite different ways of determining its worth in dollar terms: *Market value,* which is what the property would bring if it were sold today, and the *tax assessment,* the value used by your local government to calculate real es-

tate taxes. The latter is usually a percentage of the market value, but some other method may be used in your locality.

5. This item is explained in the notes (note II, page 164)—always a good place to look first for explanations. A deferred expense is an asset since it reduces current liabilities. (As I warned you, accountants have a logic all their own.)

6. *Accounts payable* are unpaid bills in hand. *Accrued expenses* are other payments that will be falling due in the immediate future, like mortgage payments.

7. The portion of the mortgage *principal* to be repaid in the coming year. You'll also have to pay interest, of course— a sum often much larger than the principal payment.

8. The mortgage principal remaining at the end of the coming year.

9. More accounting hocus-pocus. The page headed "Statement of Changes in Financial Position" shows where these figures came from.

THE PINES OWNERS ASSOCIATION, INC.
Statement of Operating Income and Expenses
For the Year Ended December 31, 1989

Income

Maintenance	$305,875
Less:	
Contribution to mortgage amortization ❶	(7,266)
Net maintenance	298,609
Interest earned	14,112
Miscellaneous ❷	5,648
TOTAL INCOME:	318,369

Expenses

Maintenance salaries and fringes	37,897
Fuel	37,046
Electricity and gas	10,139
Repairs and service contracts	24,482
Supplies	9,926
Insurance	25,010
Telephone	1,935
Depreciation & amortization ❸	44,346
Miscellaneous	1,892
TOTAL OPERATING EXPENSES:	343,179
Net loss before income taxes ❹	(24,810)
Income tax expense ❺	(6,931)
NET LOSS:	(31,741)

See accompanying notes to the financial statements.

Statement of Operating Income and Expenses

This page shows where the association's money came from and where it went. It's both the easiest part of the financial report to understand and the one you should study most closely. Get out last year's statement and compare figures from year to year. If some expenditures are up or down sharply, ask the treasurer for an explanation at the membership meeting. Except as noted below, these are all real numbers that can be interpreted in the same way as figures in your own checkbook. (Refer to reference numbers.)

1. This money was turned into a capital asset by paying off part of the mortgage and was therefore not available for regular operating expenses.

2. Typical "miscellaneous" income includes payments from concessionaires, like the laundry equipment company, and refunds from vendors in the event of an overpayment or an earned discount.

3. This is *not* a "real" cash expense but merely an estimate of the value lost through "wear and tear" on the building and equipment. The notes explain how it's calculated.

4. Before you panic at the sight of this substantial loss, look back at that "Depreciation and Amortization" item, and you'll see that this is a "paper" loss. On a *cash* basis, the building ran a surplus of $12,605, after taxes. In other words, you wound up with more money in the bank at the end of the year than in the beginning.

5. How can you owe taxes when you ran at a loss? Well, the 1987 tax reform law tightened the rules regarding the "nonrelated income" of co-ops, condominiums, and similar organizations. Briefly put, it prohibits using depreciation losses to offset income from any source other than payments from owners. As a result, all other income—from concessionaires, from commercial tenants, from interest on the reserve account—is subject to tax.

THE PINES OWNERS ASSOCIATION, INC.
Statement of Changes in Stockholders' Equity
For the Year Ended December 31, 1989

	Capital Stock ❶	Additional Paid-in Capital ❷	Retained Earnings ❸
Opening balance	$3,497	$173,357	$(54,376)
Net loss			(31,741)
Contribution to mortgage amortization		7,266	
Ending Balance	$3,497	$180,623	$(86,117)

See accompanying notes to the financial statements.

Statement of Changes in Stockholders' Equity

This page shows how the accountants determined the book value of shares in the co-operative corporation. These figures have *nothing* to do with the actual market value of your holdings; this is determined by real estate values in your community. (Refer to reference numbers.)

1. The arbitrary value assigned to shares of stock when issued, typically $1. Some shares have no par value.
2. The working capital fund set up when the co-op began, plus accumulated amortization of the mortgage.
3. Accumulated losses, including depreciation write-offs, from the time the co-op began operations.

THE PINES OWNERS ASSOCIATION, INC.
Statement of Changes in Financial Position
For the Year Ended December 31, 1989

SOURCES OF FUNDS

From Operations
Net loss	$(31,741)
Items not requiring cash	44,346
(Depreciation & amortization)	
Cash provided from operations ❶	12,605

Other Sources
Increase in accounts payable ❷	27,682
Increase in corporate taxes payable ❸	5,132
Increase in additional paid-in capital ❹	7,266
Decrease in prepaid expenses ❺	5,726
TOTAL SOURCES OF CASH:	58,411

USES OF FUNDS

Repayment of long-term debt ❻	7,266
Increase in accounts receivable ❼	1,852
Increase in mortgage escrow ❽	24,511
Additions to building ❾	82,576
TOTAL USES OF CASH:	116,205

DECREASE IN CASH ❿	(57,794)
(Excess of cash used over sources of cash)	
CASH BALANCE, BEGINNING OF YEAR	295,590
CASH BALANCE, END OF YEAR	$237,796

See accompanying note to financial statements.

Statement of Changes in Financial Position

This page compares major categories from year to year, showing trends worth keeping an eye on. It also shows how the accountants "proved" the accuracy and consistency of the figures. (Refer to reference numbers.)

1. This changes your net loss on the Statement of Operating Income and Expenses into a cash surplus, as I explained in my notes there.

2. If you don't pay your bills, you have more cash on hand. A large increase, however, may indicate that your bills are not being paid promptly; the treasurer should investigate. A decrease may indicate that your maintenance charges are not high enough to meet expenses.

3. A large change here could reflect a change in the tax laws or a substantial increase in your "nonrelated" income.

4. In most cases, amortization of the underlying mortgage.

5. Changes here have the same sources—and the same potential meaning—as those in item 2 above.

6. Mortgage *principal* again.

7. An increase here means you're carrying more "slow-pay" owners. If the trend keeps up, you should impose or increase a late payment fee or consider acceleration (see page 103) to encourage prompt payment.

8. This is a special fund set up by the bank that holds your mortgage. You make regular payments into it, and the bank uses these funds to pay your property taxes. As you might suspect, the bank is not acting for your convenience but to be sure that there will be no tax liens on the building should you default on the loan. The escrow fund usually grows rapidly in the early years of a loan, as the bank builds up a hedge against future tax increases. If the surplus seems excessive—if, on the day after the latest tax payment was made, the account still has enough money for the next two tax payments—ask the bank about refunding some of the money and reducing your required escrow payments.

9. Major improvements to the building. In this case, The Pines got a new roof.

10. Here, the decrease in cash can be accounted for by

"Additions to building": the Board took money out of the cash reserve to pay for long-term improvements. If the "Decrease in Cash" had resulted solely from operating expenses, this would be a sign of inadequate maintenance charges. If there is a substantial "Increase in Cash," the Board should transfer funds to the reserve account to provide for emergencies or future improvements.

THE PINES OWNERS ASSOCIATION, INC.
Notes to Financial Statements
Year Ended December 31, 1989

Note I. *Organization*

The Pines Owners Association, Inc. (the Corporation), was organized on March 31, 1985, as a cooperative housing corporation. On April 23, 1986, the premises known as The Pines, located at 2753 Forest Avenue, Condoville, was conveyed by Housing Solutions, Inc., to the Corporation. The building contains eighty-four (84) residential units.

Note II. *Summary of Significant Accounting Policies*

Depreciation. Depreciation is calculated using the following methods for book and income-tax purposes:

Description	Method	Life
Building	Straight Line	18 years
Boiler	Straight Line	18 years

Amortization. Expenses incurred in connection with refinancing the Corporation mortgage loans have been deferred and are being amortized over the life of the new mortgage, five (5) years.

Note III. *Mortgage Payable*

On September 17, 1987, the corporation paid off its existing obligations to the Condoville National Bank. This was done by acquiring a new mortgage from the Madison Savings Bank for $750,000 for five (5) years at 10%. The maturities for the remaining term of the loan are:

1988	$ 8,027
1989	8,867
1990	9,796
1991	714,900

The mortgage may be extended by the corporation for an additional five (5) years, provided such request is made between 90 and 120 days prior to maturity.

Note IV. *Income Tax Expense*

Real estate cooperatives are subject to Section 277 of the Internal Revenue Code. Section 277 provides that a membership organization that is operated to provide services to members is permitted to deduct expenses attributable to the furnishing of services to the members only to the extent of the income derived during such year from its members. Section 277 permits a membership organization to reduce income from nonmembership sources only by expenses incurred in generating this income. Accordingly, income from nonmembership sources such as interest, commercial rental, professional apartment rental, etc., in excess of expenses properly attributable thereto, are subject to federal tax.

Federal and state income tax expense was determined under Section 277 of the code and related state and local tax laws.

ADAM & CHECKUM
Certified Public Accountants
1234 Main Street, Condoville, USA

April 2, 1990

To the Shareholders of
The Pines Owners Association, Inc.

We have examined the balance sheet of The Pines Owners Association, Inc., as of December 31, 1989 and the related statements of income and changes in stockholders' equity and changes in financial position for the year then ended. Our examination was made in conformity with generally accepted auditing standards, and accordingly included such tests of the accounting records and such other auditing procedures as we considered necessary in the circumstances.

In our opinion, the above-mentioned financial statements present fairly the financial position of The Pines Owners Association, Inc., at December 31, 1989, and the results of its operations and changes in the financial position for the year then ended, in conformity with generally accepted accounting principles.

(signed) Adam & Checkum

The Letter of Opinion

This letter should be the first or last page of the report and should be phrased almost word for word like the sample. The phrase "in conformity with generally accepted accounting principles" must appear, verbatim, or the audit is worthless. If you see a sentence like "We were unable to determine _____ because of inadequate accounting controls" or if the sentence beginning "In our opinion" contains the word "except," there is a serious flaw in your financial record-keeping which should be corrected as quickly as possible. Ask the accountants to conduct a preliminary audit early in the next fiscal year to be sure the problem has been solved.

An unqualified audit is reassuring, but remember that the accountants are testifying only to the *accuracy of the records.* They are *not analyzing the meaning* of the figures. Questions about financial policy (Why are our payroll expenses so high? What sort of service contracts do we pay for? Do other buildings in the neighborhood have similar expenses?) should be directed to the treasurer and the board, not the accountant!

FINDING ANSWERS TO COMMON QUESTIONS: A QUICK REFERENCE

This chapter has taken you on a "grand tour" of the key documents. Often, however, you're not interested in taking the whole trip but simply in finding one particular piece of information that's of concern to you at a particular time. So here's a list of common questions and shortcuts to tell you where to start looking for the answers. There is a wide variation in local laws and customs, and even in the personal style of the sponsors who draw up these documents, so not all these shortcuts will work for all documents, but they should get you pointed in the right direction.

Who fixes what? By far the most common question that arises in shared-ownership developments. The "Definitions" section of a condo declaration or a co-op's proprietary lease should spell out the division of responsibility in detail. (See also page 126.)

How are board members elected? How are board vacancies filled? Voting procedures are spelled out in the section headed "Board of Managers" (or whatever your local term might be) in a condo's regulations or a co-op's corporate by-laws. (See also page 145.)

What restrictions affect my right to sell my unit? To rent it? Look for the subheads "Resales" and "Rentals" in the "Powers of the Board of Managers" section of your condo regulations. In a co-op, the corresponding headings, generally found in the proprietary lease, are "Assignment of Shares" and "Subletting."

May I keep pets? When is the laundry room open? These are questions answered in the house rules or community regulations.

How large a financial reserve do we have? Is it growing or shrinking? Check the page of your financial report headed "Statement of Changes in Financial Position" for a summary of your cash position and any changes that occurred in the previous year. For tracing longer trends, you'll need to look at the corresponding page from earlier statements.

Where do I complain about service problems? You may find a procedure outlined in the house rules, though this matter is often arranged on an *ad hoc* basis; contact the building manager if you're uncertain. In addition, the annual report, discussed in the next chapter, should contain the names and unit numbers of board members.

While the documents discussed here are legally required, there are others you might want to create yourself to improve communications and enhance the sense of community in your development. That's what the next chapter is about.

7

Talking to Your Neighbors:

Creating Your Internal Documents

While the formal documents are drawn up for you—by the sponsor, by a lawyer, by your accountants—there are documents you create yourself which can be equally important to running a successful shared-interest community: those in which members speak to each other. Here are some samples, designed to suggest ways in which this kind of valuable communication can take place.

NEWSLETTER

The most common and most useful means of communication within a shared-ownership development, the newsletter can serve as a means for announcing social events and introducing newcomers, calling owners meetings and reporting the results of elections, reminding residents of rules, updating owners on projects underway, and more. Ideally, it should appear at regular intervals, so that residents come to expect it and depend on it as a source of information. In a large complex, a volunteer editor and staff might produce a handsomely designed and printed monthly. In a smaller condo, one of the board members might agree to prepare a one- or two-page report, copy it, and distribute it on a bimonthly or quarterly basis. Here's a sample of such a concise, informal newsletter to suggest a format and an approach.

December, 1990

Holiday Party!

The annual tree-trimming will be held this week in the main lobby. The board will supply the tree, soda, juice, and materials for homemade ornaments. Contributions of additional refreshments or decorations are welcome. Watch the bulletin board for details. Come join us in getting the building ready to celebrate the festive season.

Work in Progress: An Update

Why is the painting taking so long? The contractor has offered us an especially favorable price in return for allowing him to take his crew off the job from time to time to complete more pressing jobs elsewhere. As a result, the work has involved alternating periods of activity and inactivity. All work (including touch-up of older problems and repainting the front doors) should be finished by mid-January.

Why were the trash chutes closed? We are installing new, more efficient compactors and improved sprinkler systems; this work required the temporary closure of the trash chutes. Now that the work is completed, the new compactors will reduce odors and pests; they will also free the porter to devote more time to cleaning the building. Now it's up to you to help us

Put a Cleaner Building in the Bag!

To maintain cleanliness and reduce odors, please *place all garbage in plastic bags* (the shopping bags supplied by local supermarkets are ideal) and *drop all bags down the chute.* Bags of garbage too large to fit must be carried to the trash cans in the basement; left on the floor, they draw pests that could soon infest *your* apartment. Newspapers and magazines *only* may be left in the service closet for the porter to carry away.

Welcome Our Youngest Newcomer

Bernard William Burton arrived November 28th, adding a special touch of joy to the holidays for Andy and Mary Burton. All good wishes to the whole family!

Late Charge Imposed

Effective in January, any owner whose monthly payment is not received by the tenth of the month will be subject to a late charge of $25. This charge was, in fact, voted two years ago but was not implemented by our previous managing agent.

We thank the vast majority of owners for their timely payments and hope this policy will end the small but persistent problem of arrears.

Policy on Repairs Clarified

The chief engineer will continue to perform minor repairs for all owners as part of his regular duties. If the cost of the materials used exceeds $10, however, the owner will be billed for the actual cost of supplies. For example, there will be no charge for replacing a washer, but an entirely new faucet will cost about $40.

For major repairs (such as replacing an entire sink), shareholders are free to engage outside contractors or make arrangements for the engineer to perform such work on his own time. Where a "building system" is involved (generally, anything *inside* a wall), the Association will bear responsibility for repairs, as provided in the Regulations.

Neighborhood Dining: Sheila's Café

The latest addition to the local dining scene (at 625 Orange Street) is a delightful blend of home-style recipes and sophisticated cooking. The atmosphere is relaxed and informal, with hardwood tables, mixed antique chairs, and paintings by local artists on the softly lit, ochre-colored walls. Owner Sheila Barnett (who lives just a block away on Menape Avenue) knows how to send a humble meat loaf to heaven with a wonderfully fresh tomato sauce. The French-style Roast Chicken with Garlic is another example of simply prepared and simply delicious food. The soups are made fresh every day; the lentil is especially soul-warming these winter nights. And save room for the desserts: the streusel-topped apple tart with hard sauce is what the all-American fruit was intended for, and the carrot cake is moist, fragrant, and virtually crackling with pecans. The breads and pastries are baked on the premises and are also available for takeout from the counter in the front.

In short, Sheila's Café is not only a welcome alternative to cooking yourself, it's a great place to spend a special evening, too. Reservations are recommended on the weekends; phone 555-2773.

HANDBOOK

A condo handbook is a convenient summary of the basic rules and organization of your association. Like some of the earlier chapters of this book, it addresses the most commonly asked questions: What, exactly, do I own? Who fixes what? How do I make a request for service? Who makes policy, and how is it changed? A summary of the house rules is usually included, as is practical information like pool and laundry room hours, parking regulations, and emergency phone numbers. Some associations make pool or parking permits part of the handbook, to be sure everyone picks up at least one copy. Such a handbook is particularly useful in resort areas, where part-time residents and a succession of visitors are often the rule; the booklet becomes the easiest way to acquaint the newcomers with the essentials of the condo's policy.

BOARD MINUTES

It's always a good practice—one often required by the governing charter—to keep minutes of each board meeting. These minutes should be available for inspection by any member of the association and by prospective buyers, their lawyers, and bankers.

Traditionally, minutes are written as a narrative of

what actually happened, summarizing virtually every statement made. While there's nothing wrong with this approach, a more concise form—like the samples that follow—is equally satisfactory. This particular secretary was a computer buff who used the machine to highlight key issues and discussions. Such a format makes it much easier to search for particular votes or resolutions when looking back through previous minutes. Even in longer narrative minutes, it's advisable to use subheads, indentations, or similar "flags" to make it easier to research past board actions. And it's surprising how often the need arises—in the interests of continuity and consistency—to examine past actions.

MINUTES

Place :	**Apt. 2043**
Date:	**Friday, March 18**
Time:	**7:30 PM**
Attended:	**Urra McClienton**
	Rosaura Diez
	James Alright
	Ulla Danavey

- **Meeting with family buying Apt. 1604 in auction:**
Paine Lamme Lin Ma
Mary Uptight
Rosa Y. Seart (co-borrower)

  They were informed that co-borrower may not reside in Apt. They were asked for copies of income-tax returns not provided.

- **Joseph Alfred check re Koop's fee, which was returned (NSF). It was decided that the co-op will use Alfred's services only as presently needed.**

- **The Fannegans presented a pro forma invoice on proposed design changes to lobby and surrounding areas.**

MINUTES

Place:	Apt. 1756
Date:	Tuesday, April 19
Time:	7:30 PM
Attended:	Urra McClienton
	Rosaura Diez
	Elisha Wordson

- **Voted on purchase on Apt. 1604 as follows:**

YES	NO
Urra McClienton	
Rosaura Diez	
Elisha Wordson	
James Alright (absent)	
Ulla Danavey (absent)	
3	0

Rosaura will contact Ira with the decision.
Agreement will specify that niece cannot live in Apt. and that he cannot lease it.

- **Sink has been installed in laundry room.**

- **Ida McClienton cleaned studio in basement area.**

- **Apt. 404 is still having leaks. Urra will call Zeus Corp. about repairs. Apt. 304 is showing water damage to bathroom wall and window.**

- **Zeus Corp. has been consulted on estimates for needed plumbing work. They promise there will be no need to cut off water evenings or nights.**

- **Paperwork on Shwigs contract will be distributed to Board members by E. Wordson as soon as it's completed.**

THE ANNUAL REPORT

One of the most useful types of communication from the board to the unit owners is a summary of past and proposed actions. Not only does it allow the owners to understand how their money is being spent—and what additional expenses can be foreseen for the future—it also provides the annual meetings with a useful focus, ensuring that no important points get overlooked.

The sample that follows is from a building only recently converted to shared ownership and therefore undergoing considerable upgrading. Reports in other complexes may be shorter or longer, depending on the physical condition of the property and the nature and extent of board activities.

STATE OF THE BUILDING

The Board of Directors has made a special effort over the past two years to assess building systems and determine areas in need of immediate, near-term, and long-term attention. This report, itemizing the key priorities we have established, is designed to serve three purposes: to show unit owners the nature of the problems we confront, to explain why some projects can be undertaken now while others must be postponed, and to show that regular increases in maintenance charges will be essential to continue a program of improvements.

Some key facts should be kept in mind. First of all, the building is nearly 50 years old, and normal wear and tear are taking their toll; routine upkeep for such a structure inevitably requires substantial sums. Furthermore, our building, like many others in this area, has suffered the effects of "deferred maintenance" (i.e., neglect). In restoring services to a superior level, therefore, we find ourselves confronting a number of "catch-up" expenses as well as normal upkeep.

ROOFING

WHAT IT IS: Our roof consists of two layers of tarred felt, covered with a loose, gravel-like substance called slag. This is a durable type of construction which has held up pretty well for several decades. It has two drawbacks: (1) When a spot begins to sag or fail, the slag tends to trap water at the weak point, hastening the development of leaks, and (2) when repair or replacement becomes necessary, costs are high, since the slag must be raked up and carried off.

WHAT'S WRONG? The roof has developed several leaks, some severe, especially in an area damaged by a fire about ten years ago. The situation has been stabilized by temporary patching, but replacement in the near future is essential. Repairing the roof is an essential precondition to any other reconstruction work, since continuing leakage will damage any other repaired elements.

WHAT SHOULD BE DONE? The definitive—and costly—solution is a new roof. It would carry a written guarantee from the contractor, sparing us any future roof expense for at least a decade. The new roof would also afford better insulation, and modern materials would be less costly to repair in the future.

PRIORITY: Urgent

ESTIMATED COST: $195,000

WINDOWS

SURVEY RESULTS: The survey conducted by our team of volunteer shareholders covered about 80% of our 780 windows. The principal findings are that nearly all windows require some mechanical repairs, and 35% should be completely replaced. Upper-floor windows are in generally worse shape than those on lower floors (the roof problems are an important factor here); otherwise the condition of windows varies more or less at random throughout the building. (The time, effort, and money devoted to them over the years by various tenants seems to be the decisive factor.) As a result, the option of replacing only the worst windows and repairing others would be difficult to carry out without appearing to shortchange some unit owners. Furthermore, the cost of this option is roughly equal to that of premium aluminum windows for the entire building, and total replacement would immediately place all unit owners on an equal footing.

PRACTICAL CONSIDERATIONS: Wood replacement windows would best preserve the building's appearance, but the cost would be 40% (roughly $100,000) higher than any other option. Given our other needs, this is beyond the reach of our budget. In addition, wood windows are more difficult to clean and require regular painting. Premium nonwood replacements offer good appearance and considerable convenience.

WHAT COMES NEXT? We are seeking bids on the aluminum replacement and reconstruction/repair options and will implement the most attractive proposal.

PRIORITY: Urgent

ESTIMATED COST: $200,000–$225,000

COMPACTORS

WHERE THEY ARE, WHAT THEY DO: A compactor stands at the bottom of the trash chute in each wing. By reducing the volume of refuse that needs to be stored between collections, the compactor makes garbage easier to handle and helps control odor and pests. This efficiency could free the porter to do other cleaning and maintenance tasks. Sprinklers, which are part of the compactor system, prevent trash fires.

WHAT'S WRONG WITH THEM? Our compactors are poorly built, poorly maintained, and have not been in working order in years. In a recent fire department inspection, we failed.

WHAT WILL WE DO? Their poor condition and outdated design make the compactors unlikely candidates for repair, so replacement is the only viable option.

PRIORITY: Now under way

ESTIMATED COST: $12,000

PAINTING

WHAT'S WRONG? It has been several years since the hallways were painted, and it shows. The entranceway and doors desperately need attention. Minor repairs and the reconstruction of the elevators have created new eyesores throughout the building.

PRIORITY: Now under way

ESTIMATED COST: $17,000

ASBESTOS

WHERE IT IS AND WHAT IT DOES: Steam and hot water pipes in the basement are insulated with asbestos padding, which has begun to deteriorate.

WHAT'S WRONG? Asbestos fiber, once a standard insulating material, has been shown to cause cancer when inhaled regularly. As a result, health and safety codes now require that existing asbestos be removed or encapsulated. Luckily, there is relatively little asbestos in our building, none in areas where people live, and experts agree that stable, undisturbed asbestos presents the smallest risk. Nevertheless, we are compelled by law to develop a plan for removing it.

WHAT CAN BE DONE? The cleanup can be undertaken only be a specialized contractor. Costs are considerable, since every trace of asbestos must be removed, and precautions must be taken to keep dust from spreading beyond the affected areas. While no emergency exists, this project must be factored into our plans.

PRIORITY: Intermediate term

OTHER ACTIONS

In addition to the ongoing projects described above, the Board of Trustees has taken these actions in the course of the past year:

- Undertaken the complete reconstruction of the elevators, including the negotiation of a new maintenance contract. (Total cost: $110,000)
- Engaged our first outside managing agent. While this experience has proved unsatisfactory in some respects, it has brought active day-to-day management to the building and has enabled the resident Board members to gain a better understanding of the association's needs.

We now understand the requirements (and costs) of more aggressive maintenance, the full extent of the responsibilities that will eventually devolve to the resident unit owners, and the ways residents can take a more active role in running the association's affairs. This report is itself an example of the insights gained from the change.

COMMUNITY GUIDE

A great convenience to newcomers, and a handy device for getting more residents involved in neighborhood activities, a community guide can be prepared by the board or an ad hoc committee. The next page shows the table of contents and some sample entries from one such guide.

Obviously, there's a lot of room for "customizing" here. If there are many young families in your building, make a special effort to scout out day-care centers, children's theaters, and other activities that might particularly interest them. If there are a number of singles who don't have time to cook, look for attractive, moderately priced restaurants. Be sure to tap the expertise of long-term residents to learn about those "special" shops in out-of-the-way corners. And don't overlook the informational assets of the organizations you list in the guide. A local minister may be able to give you a list of all the local religious organizations, and a local chamber of commerce could supply a directory of local merchants.

To be an ongoing success, a guide needs updating at least once a year. Try to get one person—the chair of the communications committee, for example—to take on the responsibility, perhaps aided by an ad hoc committee. Ideally, the updaters should have access to a computer, which makes the work so much easier!

COMMUNITY GUIDE

Suggestions from your neighbors. This listing is not intended to be exhaustive; additions for future editions are always welcome.

Table of Contents

EMERGENCY SERVICES

SHOPPING
   Supermarkets
   Convenience stores
   Greengrocers
   Fish markets
   Dry cleaners

Hardware stores
Antiques

ENTERTAINMENT
Restaurants & takeouts
Community theaters
Movie theaters

CHURCHES
BAPTIST
CONGREGATIONAL
EPISCOPAL
LUTHERAN
METHODIST
PRESBYTERIAN
ROMAN CATHOLIC
SEVENTH DAY ADVENTIST

SYNAGOGUES

PUBLIC SERVICES
Post Offices
Elected Officials
Transportation

Sample Listing:

Supermarkets:

GOLDEN FOOD (555–1858)
367 Wilson Avenue (between Longacre & Gresham, 1 block
east)
Hours: Mon-Wed & Sat, 8–6:45, Thurs & Fri, 8–7:45; Sun
9–2:45
Closest and smallest of the neighborhood supermarkets.

SUPREME CHOICE (555–8656)
325 Longacre Avenue (Grand Avenue, 4 blocks east)
Hours: Mon–Wed & Sat, 8–7:45; Thurs & Fri, 8–8:45; Sun
9–3:45
Large, modern store.

Talking to Your Neighbors 183

BAKER'S (555–8245)
492 Million Avenue (Henderson Street, 3 blocks north, 3 east)
Hours: Mon–Fri, 8–9:45; Sat, 8–7:45; Sun, 9–4:45
Large selection, convenient hours.

ELECTED OFFICIALS:

MAYOR'S COMPLAINT HOTLINE (555–0800)
This is designed to be the "citizen's shortcut" to city services; they can help you track down the office responsible for solving your problem, but you'll have to follow up yourself.

PATRICIA WILLIAMS, Council Member (555–1290)
405 Longacre Avenue
Ms. Williams' staff is available during normal office hours to deal with complaints. She was highly supportive of our tax appeal last year; you might want to thank her for this concern if you write.

CHARLES LUDLOW, 12th District Representative
150 Main Street (555–9078)
You can also address the Congressman at his Washington office: Longworth Office Building, Washington, DC 20525.

Sen. Edward De Vries
123 Second Street (555–6767)

Sen. John Manley
255 Barton Street (555–4040)
You can also address our senators in their Washington offices: Dirksen Office Building, Washington, DC 20535

8

Home Sweet Condo

Making the Most of Shared Ownership

At this point, you are probably beginning to wonder if buying into a shared-ownership development is such a great idea after all. There's financial risk, there are a lot of rules to deal with, and there's a lot of work to do. Isn't there a simpler way? Well, you could rent—and give up the tax benefits, the financial security, and the other privileges that come with home ownership. You could buy a house of your own—and have to face the higher costs, while coping with the headaches of regular maintenance entirely on your own. While shared ownership is not perfect, for millions of families, it's the most attractive option in today's housing market. Above and beyond the financial advantages, it offers some distinctive pluses.

First of all, you do indeed own the property. You and the neighbors you see everyday—*and no one else*—make the key decisions: what priorities to establish for service and repairs, whether the basement should be used as a storage room or as a recreation room for the kids, whether the grounds should be as neat as a golf course or as natural as a wooded glen.

The money you invest in making your home more comfortable and attractive is money you can recover if you ever choose to move. Install a built-in bookcase in a rental apartment, and you've bought a gift for the landlord. Do the same in a condo, and you've enhanced the resale value of your property. There's no need to settle for a Cheap-O refrigerator, when the Grande Luxe frost-free with built-in ice-maker you buy now is yours to keep, either to sell it when you move or take it along.

And while being a joint owner does entail some occasionally difficult negotiations, it also has a strong positive side. If a pipe bursts while you're on vacation in the Caribbean, there are your fellow owners and, often, a professional staff to handle emergency repairs in your absence. When your property needs a major repair, you have other, equally interested people to help with the research and evaluation needed to make a wise choice—and also to help pay the cost. Finally, when you call a contractor, you're not just one person but an association—a bigger customer with potentially more clout.

Then there are the intangible advantages. Shared ownership provides a structure for getting to know your neighbors and for working with them on projects of common interest. What starts out as a discussion of how to finance a pool heater may turn into a lively working committee organizing a rummage sale. Strike up a conversation with the person seated next to you at a membership meeting, and you may discover that one of your neighbors shares your fascination with modern dance. In an age when we so often find ourselves living in a closed world, sealed in with the TV and the CD, the shared-ownership structure helps develop a sense of community—especially welcome in a large, impersonal city, but a good feeling anywhere.

Capitalizing on these advantages entails a bit of effort, but it's the kind of effort that can be fun. Take part in social events, and, if you enjoy planning, cooking, or decorating, contribute to them. Chat with the neighbors you encounter in the hall, at the pool, or in the laundry room; if you discover common interests, think about ways to share them. If you enjoy cooking, why not extend a dinner invitation? If it's biking you enjoy, why not see if other residents want to join you for a weekly ride? Some delightful additions to your social life may be right next door.

Taking an active role in the community can ease the

inevitable burdens of shared ownership, too. To keep the financial risks within reasonable limits, take the time to read your association's financial statements and ask questions about anything you don't understand. The sooner problems are discovered and resolved, the less costly they will be. To keep time demands within reasonable limits, offer your help in whatever area you have expertise. If finance is your specialty, offer to serve on the audit committee. If you enjoy writing, offer to serve on the newsletter committee. If you'd like to get even more involved, run for the board. Running a shared-ownership development is definitely a case of "many hands making light work."

Of course, even with the best of will and the kindest of neighbors, there will be conflicts and setbacks, but with patience they can usually be resolved. If a meeting threatens to turn into a shouting match, just call it off. Let everyone reconsider before you try again to deal with the divisive issue, whatever it may be. To paraphrase Ben Franklin, you need to hang together, or your housing and family finances will surely hang separately.

In fact, a condo or co-op is a microcosm of American society: a highly diverse group of people seeking to improve their lives by stressing their common interests and turning their differences into sources of mutual strength. Living in a shared-interest complex provides a chance to observe and participate in this unique process. Best of all, it gives you the opportunity to sit in your living room as master of all you survey, enjoying the special satisfaction of owning your own home sweet condo.

Index